Best Eas...

D0720008

Best Easy Day Hikes
Santa Fe

Second Edition

Linda Black Regnier
and
Katie Regnier

FALCONGUIDE®

GUILFORD, CONNECTICUT
HELENA, MONTANA
AN IMPRINT OF THE GLOBE PEQUOT PRESS

To buy books in quantity for corporate use
or incentives, call **(800) 962–0973, ext. 4551,**
or e-mail **premiums@GlobePequot.com.**

Contents

Overview Map

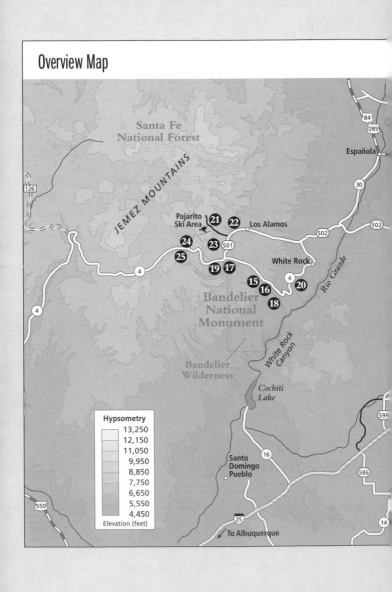

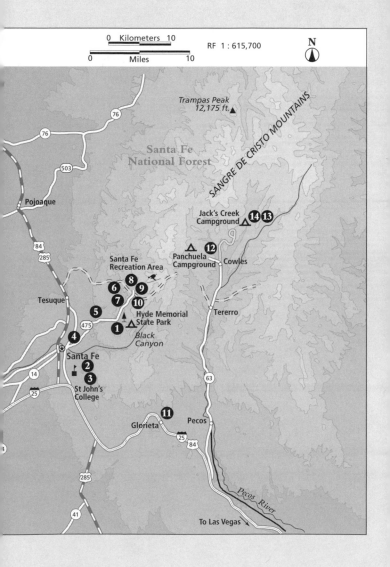

Acknowledgments

From its inception, we have shared this venture with our family. This second edition became more of a family affair, as Katie has moved on in her career and couldn't accompany me on all the hikes, and Jim Regnier, my husband, took over where she left off. Not only was Jim my hiking companion but GPS technician and chief mechanic for our new pickup camper, our home away from home. We continued to depend on the support of our entire family: Krisi; Annie; Hope; Thalin; our new little kid, Drew; and our new big kid, Mitch, Katie's husband.

We also have friends to thank. Judy Fay and Phil Campbell accompanied us through rain, sleet, hail, and snow as we caravanned our way from Montana to New Mexico. I promised them beautiful March weather, but it was not to be! They persevered, and thanks to their suggestions, we have incorporated several new and easier hikes. Jean Templeton also traveled to Santa Fe from Maine and was wonderful company along old and new trails.

Once again, the rangers at Hyde State Park were friendly and helpful. Ranger Joe was surprised to see us again, after a seven-year absence, and ranger naturalist Mike was our resource for the Circle Trail. Richard Atkinson of the New Mexico Public Lands Information Center was knowledgeable and helpful, as he was for our first edition. We found a great new source of expertise in Greg Ohlsen of Travel Bug, Santa Fe.

Our thanks to all.

Ranking the Hikes

Easiest → More Difficult

Introduction

Climb the mountains and get their glad tidings. Nature's peace will flow into you as the sunshine flows into the trees. The winds blow their freshness into you and the storms their energy while cares drop away like the leaves of autumn.

— John Muir

In this second edition we hope, once again, to share some of the wilderness of northern New Mexico with you. It is our sincere wish that this exposure will encourage you to help with efforts to conserve this precious resource for all of us and for those who follow.

The most comforting thing about returning "home" to northern New Mexico year after year is that some things never change. Most notable for me is the view across the Rio Grande Valley, from the Jemez to the Sangre de Cristo Mountains. It is etched in my psyche from childhood, and it fills my heart with memories. However, since the writing of the first edition of this book, much has changed. There is development in what I had considered the most remote places, and even more distressing is the widespread toll that the drought and the infestation of pine beetle has had on the landscape. This lethal combination has left vast areas of piñon, ponderosa pine, and Douglas fir gray and lifeless.

After considering the feedback we received, we have revised our definition of "easy" and have incorporated several new hikes, while eliminating others. There are intriguing new destinations and also geological wonders such as the Valles Caldera National Preserve. We have also updated trail descriptions, necessitated by the effects of fire and erosion and routine changes in trail markers. We have also eliminated trailheads that were difficult to access without high-clearance vehicles and were problematic in foul weather.

We have attempted to give accurate mileage for all hikes; however, in spite of recent GPS developments, often the coverage is inaccurate in heavily forested areas. Therefore, we have consulted other resources and have calculated as closely as possible the length of each hike. Also note that elevation change is a different value than cumulative elevation gain. Elevation change indicates the lowest elevation and highest elevation encountered during the hike. Read the description of each hike carefully, as there may be much more elevation gain (numerous ascents and descents) than the elevation change indicates. Set a reasonable pace (2 miles per hour is average), and be sure to take breaks each hour.

We have arranged our hikes according to five areas, all within approximately an hour's drive of Santa Fe. We have included some of the new urban trails close to Santa Fe. Although not covered in this book, this option is also available in Los Alamos. Other options range from high mountain peaks to flat mesa tops and low-lying canyons. These are unique places, offering glimpses into the geological history and human history of northern New Mexico.

Day hiking into wild places requires careful planning. Once you "get it together" in your backpack, you'll be ready to go at a moment's notice. Consider high-energy snacks along with your lunch and be sure to carry enough water. You may also want to carry a water filtration system or a water bottle with a built-in top filter. Never drink water from mountain streams or lakes without purification. Other items include: a topographical map; a good compass (that you have mastered before you set out); first-aid supplies; SPF lip balm and sunscreen; toilet paper and plastic bags; rain gear; sun hat; extra socks; sandals for stream crossings; and a pocketknife. Optional items include a couple of bandanas, which have numerous uses; hiking poles (reported to relieve as much as 30 percent of the stress on your knees); and a GPS.

For this second edition we hiked through March and April snows, spring rain, and through a considerable amount of timber downfall in the Pecos Wilderness. In May we ran into more rain and the beginning of the summer heat. Even in June there may be snowdrifts at high elevations. Therefore, it is wise to wear and carry layers of clothing. It is also wise to contact the appropriate ranger district to check on the weather. Late afternoon thunderstorms, especially in July and August, can be dangerous on mountain peaks and plateaus, and flash flooding can occur in canyons and arroyos.

Learn about wildlife you may encounter while hiking and always keep your distance. Many varieties of rattlesnakes are found in New Mexico, from desert areas to conifer forests; therefore, always be aware of where you are placing your hands and feet. Should you get bitten, it's best to get to a hospital as quickly as you can. You may also consider carrying a Sawyer venom extractor to aspirate the venom (do not use oral suction). In addition, to slow the dispersion of the venom, use an Ace bandage tied (not too tightly) on the joint nearest the bite. Stay calm and get medical attention.

Do not leave valuables in your car. Trailheads are not patrolled, and although we have selected hikes in areas we consider safer than others, there is no guarantee your car will not be vandalized. Another precaution: Be sure to inform someone of your destination and expected time of return.

As with any exercise program, take care to monitor your own physical abilities. An extremely important health precaution, before heading out on the trail in high altitudes, is to allow your body to acclimate. Rest and drink lots of water for one or two days upon arriving in Santa Fe. Know the symptoms of AMS (acute mountain sickness) and HAPE and HACE (high-altitude pulmonary edema and high-altitude cerebral edema). AMS symptoms include headache, loss of appetite, shortness of breath, insomnia, and lassitude. Rest and hydration should relieve symptoms. If not, descend immediately 1,500 to 2,000 feet. HAPE and HACE are rare but can be life-threatening. Symptoms include unbearable headache, vomiting, disorientation, hallucinations, shortness of breath, and a crackling sound in the chest. These demand an immediate descent and medical attention.

Please give attention to the "ethics" of hiking, an essential consideration in preserving our wilderness areas. All hikers have the responsibility of leaving zero impact on the environment. This involves three simple rules: Leave with everything you brought; leave no sign of your visit; leave the landscape as you found it. In the dry New Mexican terrain, it is difficult for any scrap to disintegrate, so leave nothing behind. In addition, bury your waste 6 to 8 inches deep, at least 300 feet from any water source. Be sure to pack out toilet paper.

Keep in mind that it is unlawful to remove archaeological artifacts or to disturb ruins. Even touching can be harmful to these priceless objects and locations. The soil, too, needs protection. Crytobiotic soil crust consists of a group of organisms that live on desert soils. This soil supplies nutrients to plants, absorbs and holds water, and helps prevent erosion. When crytobiotic soil is mature it becomes a lumpy black crust, but it can be almost invisible in the early stages of growth. Therefore, stay on designated trails, and if you must walk off the trail, remember to stay in dry streambeds and on bare rock. Staying on the trail and resting on durable surfaces also cuts down on erosion in this dry climate.

Don't be deterred by this litany of preparations and precautions. With careful planning, awareness, and consideration for the environment, your mind will be eased and your hiking experience matchless!

How to Use the Maps

The maps in this book depict a detailed close-up of an area and use elevation tints, called hypsometry, to portray relief. Each gray tone represents a range of equal elevation, as shown in the scale key with the map. These maps will give you a good idea of elevation gain and loss. The darker tones are lower elevations and the lighter grays are higher elevations. The lighter the tone, the higher the elevation. Narrow bands of different gray tones spaced closely together indicate steep terrain, whereas wider bands indicate areas of more gradual slope.

Map Legend

	National Monument Boundary	∩	Cave
	National Forest Boundary	)(	Pass
	State Park Boundary	▲	Elevation Peak
׀׀׀׀׀׀׀׀׀׀	Fence Line	🚶	Trailhead
──25──	Interstate	❷	Trail Locator
──84──	U.S. Highway	↻	Trail Turnaround
──475──	State Highway	🅿	Parking
──────	Primary Road	🎿	Ski Basin
──────	Other Road	🚐	RV Park
══════	Unpaved Road	▲	Campground
= = = = =	Unimproved Road	⊼	Picnic Table
▬▬▬▬▬▬	Featured Unpaved Road	🏕	Picnic Area
▬▬150▬▬	Featured Unimproved Road	○	Town
▬ ▬ ▬ ▬	Featured Trail	👁	Viewpoint
- - - - - -	Other Trail	■	Point of Interest
─ ─ ─ ─	Ski Lift	🛈	Visitor Center
∿	River/Creek	•─•	Gate
∿	Intermittent Stream	⤬	Bridge
℘	Spring		
∥	Falls		
⬬	Lake/river		

Santa Fe

Santa Fe represents a unique blend of the Spanish, Mexican, American Indian, and North American cultures, which permeates every aspect of life and activity in northern New Mexico. For happenings in Santa Fe and vicinity, consult the book *Insiders' Guide to Santa Fe*.

Urban trails have recently been developed in many cities. Santa Fe has a new system of urban trails, and two of these are included in this edition. These are wonderful early morning or evening getaways for the entire family. The remainder of the hikes closest to Santa Fe begin and end in the Sangre de Cristo Mountains. Named the "blood of Christ" because of their color at sunset, these mountains have the highest elevation of any range in New Mexico. Because of their proximity to Santa Fe, many of the hikes we've included are frequently busier after work hours, when people wish to get some quick exercise, and on weekends. The trails are well worn and well maintained and serve not only hikers but hikers and their dogs, runners, and mountain bikers.

There are numerous campgrounds north of Santa Fe on Highway 475. Black Canyon, a USDA Forest Service campground, is located in a heavily wooded and shaded area and has excellent facilities, including a campground host and the availability of reservations. At the time of updating it was undergoing renovations. There are restrooms but no electricity or showers. Hyde Memorial State Park is only 8 miles from Santa Fe and is the highest state park in New Mexico at 8,500 feet. This 350-acre park has seventy-five camping sites, seven of which are designated RV, with water and electricity. Most of the tent sites have shelters, toilets, and water nearby. We also spotted a centrally located playground. Big Tesuque is a third campground, located several miles north of Black Canyon. It is open spring through fall, and there are ten tent campsites and no fees. Aspen Vista is a picnic area a short distance north and is the trailhead for the Tesuque Peak hike.

1 Black Canyon Trail

Type of hike: Loop.
Distance: 1.5 miles, round trip.
Elevation change: 360 feet.

Maps: McClure Reservoir (USGS).

Finding the trailhead: From Santa Fe Plaza drive north on Washington Avenue. At the first light after the intersection with Paseo de Peralta, turn right onto Artist's Road, which becomes Highway 475. At approximately 7 miles turn right (east) into Black Canyon Campground. Parking is allocated for hikers outside the campground entrance. Please note that as this book was being updated, the Black Canyon Campground and Trail were closed for renovation. The previous trailhead was located at campsite number 4; however, this work may result in the relocation of the trailhead. Ask the campground host for directions or call the Espanola Ranger District at 505-753-7331. Remember that camping at this well-maintained, forested campground is a real treat!

The Hike

This hike, close to Santa Fe, is suitable for children. It is easy, well shaded, and a good introduction to mountain terrain, fir-aspen belt vegetation, and wildflowers. In early summer we found red columbine, clematis, false solomon's seal, and Oregon grape.

The first section of the hike is a gradual ascent on a wide, somewhat rocky path. At about 0.3 mile there is a fork in the trail and a wooden sign displaying a double arrow. Proceed left (southeast) for the Black Canyon Loop. The trail veers to the right (southwest) and ascends. At 0.5 mile you will reach a fork. Continue straight ahead. Be certain to stay on the trail. The watershed for Santa Fe (to your left, south, over the

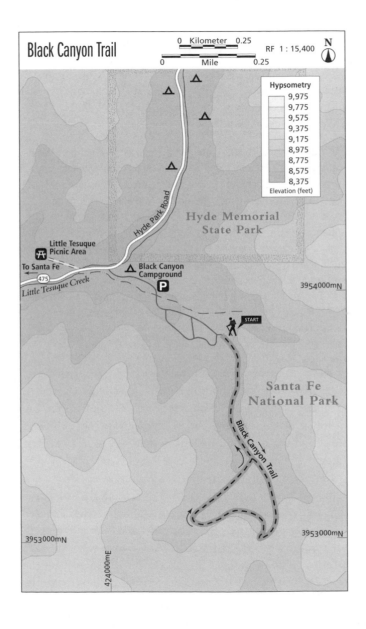

saddle) is out of bounds for hikers, and a heavy fine is imposed for trespassing. As you descend for the final part of this loop trail, you walk through a beautiful aspen grove. Soon you intersect with the original trail. Retrace your steps and finish up your hike at the campsite.

2 Santa Fe Canyon Preserve Interpretive Trail (Nature Conservancy)

Type of hike: Loop.
Distance: 1.5 miles.
Elevation change: 100 feet.

Maps: Dale Ball Trails Map (Travel Bug), Santa Fe Canyon Preserve Trail (Nature Conservancy).

Finding the trailhead: From the center of Santa Fe, take Canyon Road east. When it ends on East Alameda, take a right. At the first stop sign take a left onto Upper Canyon Road for 1.3 miles. Turn left as Upper Canyon Road merges with Cerro Gordo Road, just before the pavement ends. Take an immediate right into the City of Santa Fe Parks and Recreation municipal parking lot (open from 7:00 A.M. to 7:00 P.M., strictly enforced). Follow signs to the trailhead. A branch of the Dale Ball Foothill Trail system is also located here. Bikes and pets are not allowed on this trail (a different regulation from the Dale Ball Trail system).

The Hike

This is an easy walk in one of the last unspoiled riparian areas in Santa Fe. There are 190 acres of cottonwoods, willows, and other native species, which provide an excellent

Santa Fe Canyon Preserve Interpretive Trail (Nature Conservancy)

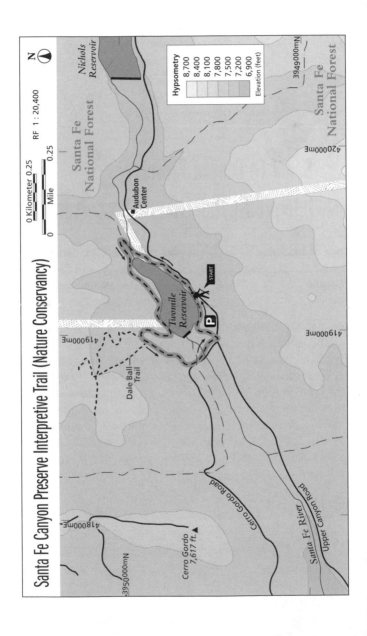

N

RF 1 : 20,400

0   Kilometer   0.25
0   Mile   0.25

Hypsometry
8,700
8,400
8,100
7,800
7,500
7,200
6,900
Elevation (feet)

Nichols Reservoir

Santa Fe National Forest

Santa Fe National Forest

Audubon Center

3949000mN

420000mE

Tuonile Reservoir

START

P

419000mE

Dale Ball Trail

Cerro Gordo Road

Santa Fe River

Upper Canyon Road

Cerro Gordo 7,617 ft. ▲

418000mE

3950000mN

opportunity for birding. For most of the twentieth century this area was the original route of the Santa Fe River and contained the reservoirs for the emerging city. There are numerous interpretative signs describing this history as well as additional in-depth ecological information.

Head northeast, up the creek bed on a well-worn trail. The signposts describe the former reservoirs, which time has returned to nature. As you continue, moisture dependent cottonwood, willow, and box elder line the riparian area. In this streamside forest (bosque), over 140 species of birds have been found.

The trail meanders beside the stream, comes to a clearing in the willows, takes a right (south) and proceeds uphill for a short distance before coming to a fork in the trail. Walk left. On your left you will see another historic marker, which describes the features of the old waterworks in front of you. Note the old pipes and water gauge. Veering to the left (north), again you will walk through a short, swampy area (in spring), and at the edge of the dam, three benches provide great resting places. The trail then heads northeast along a stone-lined path and comes to another interpretative plaque, at the 0.5 mile marker.

The Interpretive Loop follows the trail heading left (northwest) and uphill. It then turns south, along the old metal retaining wall above the reservoir. When the wall ends, follow the well-marked trail as it curves north through a gate and then heads through dry arroyos and piñon hillsides. It winds southwest, and you will pass the hydroelectric plant on your left. Go through a gate and you find yourself on Cerro Gordo Road, where the parking area is located. Turn left and the parking lot is just a short walk.

3 Dorothy Stewart Trail

Type of hike: Loop.
Distance: 2 miles.
Elevation change: 80 feet.

Maps: Dale Ball Trails Map
(available at Travel Bug).

Finding the trailhead: From downtown Santa Fe take Alameda Street east (paralleling the Santa Fe River). Turn right (south) on Camino Cabra and continue until it intersects with Camino de Cruz Blanca. Turn left (west) at this intersection and you will see St. John's College on your immediate right. Stay on Camino de Cruz Blanca for 0.7 mile. The trailhead is on your left, with parking for only three cars. There is additional parking a short distance up the road at the Atalaya Mountain trailhead.

The Hike

This trail was established through the joint efforts of the Forest Trust and the City of Santa Fe, and through the hard work of Irene Von Horvath. It is a wonderful urban hike, easy to follow on a well-maintained trail, and it gives the impression that you are far above the activity of the city. The vegetation is very representative of the Santa Fe area, and the marvelous views in all directions are at very little cost in terms of exertion. It makes an excellent sunset or evening hike in the summer; however, it can be a real scorcher during the day!

To begin, walk through the opening in the wooden fence and head straight ahead (north). Walk downhill, along gentle switchbacks; piñon, juniper, and an occasional ponderosa pine surround you. We found wonderful spring wildflowers and beautiful lichen on the granite rocks lining the

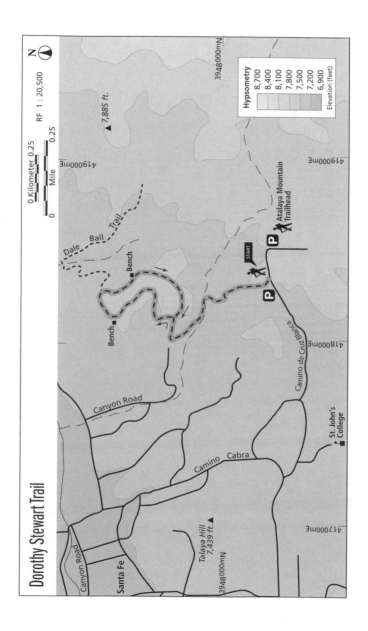

trail. At about 0.25 mile, near the bottom of a small canyon, the trail takes a turn to the left (northwest), as the sign for the Dorothy Stewart Trail indicates. Be certain to stay on the main trail (a smaller trail cuts off to the left as you begin to walk uphill).

The higher you climb, the more rewarding the views. The first distant range of mountains is the Sandia, near Albuquerque. At about 0.5 mile the trail splits left and right. We chose left (north) and the views continued to be spectacular! Suddenly, we eyed a great log and rock bench and rested with the beautiful view. At about 1 mile the Dale Ball Trail breaks off to the left (northeast). Continue straight ahead on the well-marked Dorothy Stewart Trail Loop.

Another bench appears, and this time the view is of Tesuque Peak. Continue on and you loop around the mountainside and reconnect with the original trail, which brings you back to the trailhead.

4 Dale Ball Trail–North

Type of hike: Loop.
Distance: 3.25 miles.
Elevation change: 322 feet.

Maps: Dale Ball Trails Map
(available at Travel Bug).

Finding the trailhead: From Santa Fe Plaza drive north on Washington Avenue. At the first light after the intersection with Paseo de Peralta, turn right onto Artist's Road, which becomes Highway 475 and Hyde Park Road. Drive 2.6 miles (do not measure mileage by the mile markers) to the junction with Sierra del Norte, which is on your left. Turn left and take an immediate right into the trailhead parking lot.

The Hike

Thanks to the perseverance and the hard work of Dale Ball, there is now an extensive trail system in the foothills surrounding Santa Fe. About ten years ago Ball had a dream to connect the strange pattern of city and county land, mostly on the east side of Santa Fe. He envisioned a system of trails that could be used year-round. Most of the resulting trails are on city or county land, but they are joined together by parcels of private land on permanent easements. Begun in 2000, work is hoped to be completed around the time of this guide's printing.

Dale Ball has done a great service to hikers, bikers (who constitute half of the trail usage), runners, and dog lovers (dogs must be leashed). The trails are well laid out, eliminating erosion and blind corners, and well maintained. Each has an informative activity board at the trailhead.

Because this system has been created with easements provided by private property owners, it is requested that you

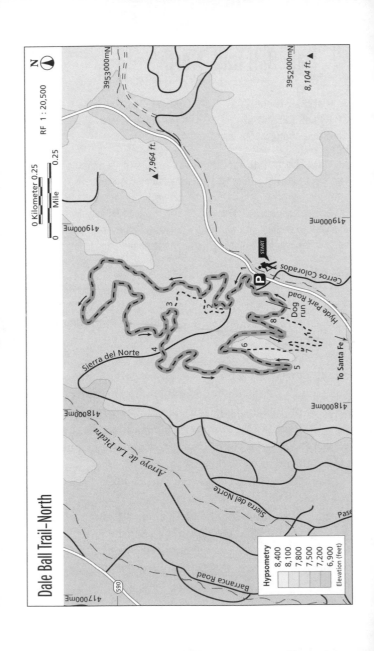

Dale Ball Trail–North

Hypsometry

Elevation (feet)
8,400
8,100
7,800
7,500
7,200
6,900

RF 1 : 20,500

0 Kilometer 0.25

0 Mile 0.25

N

stay on the trail, take no shortcuts (often the easements are only 6 feet wide), be respectful of private property, and be responsible with your dog. Having these open spaces is a privilege, which could be lost if abused.

Dale Ball hikes are easily accessed from the city, and a detailed map can be purchased at Travel Bug, 839 Paseo de Peralta, Santa Fe, 87501; (505) 922–0418.

The Dale Ball Trail–North is only one of many hiking and biking trails in the Dale Ball system. It is close to Santa Fe and gives a good introduction to the piñon and juniper hillsides, as well as the unusual and diverse seasonal flora surrounding Santa Fe. Although it meanders through private property at times, there are many spaces that seem remote and far from any neighborhood. It can be a great evening hike, but it could be very hot in the summer. Please note that there is a pet run across the street from the trailhead parking lot. Dogs are required to be leashed on the trail.

Post #1: From the north end of the parking lot, walk uphill and veer to the left (northwest) through piñon and juniper. At post #2 go right (southeast) and the trail then turns to the left (northwest). You ascend on several switchbacks and are rewarded with a clear view of the Jemez Mountains to the northwest. There is again a gentle elevation gain, and at about 0.6 mile Black Mesa (adjacent to San Ildefonso Pueblo) can be seen to the west.

This well-maintained trail meanders around the Santa Fe hills, up and down, and the higher the elevation, the better the view. At post #3 go right (south). There is an immediate downhill on long gentle switchbacks, and post #4 finds you at about 1.7 miles, crossing Sierra del Norte. Head right (north) and uphill once again. Soon you have views of Albuquerque to the south. At post #5 (the trail marker may be defaced), go left (north). You'll be rewarded with wonderful views across the Rio Grande Valley, once again. At post #6 go left (north), down a series of long switchbacks, to post #8 (eliminate #7) Here, take a left (south) and quickly return to the trailhead.

5 Chamisa Trail

Type of hike: Out-and-back.
Distance: 4.5 miles, round trip.
Elevation change: 1,200 feet.

Maps: Aspen Basin and McClure Reservoir (USGS), Pecos Wilderness (USFS).

Finding the trailhead: From Santa Fe Plaza drive north on Washington Avenue. Proceed through the intersection with Paseo de Peralta and turn right at the first light onto Artist's Road, which becomes Highway 475. At 5.6 miles there is a large parking area on the left (north). The trailhead is located at the east end of the parking lot.

The Hike

This hike is close to Santa Fe and offers a good workout as well as great exposure to piñon-juniper and mixed-conifer vegetation belts. There is lots of shade most of the day, and the reward for uphill exertion is a welcome descent into the Big Tesuque Creek basin, where you can rest amid cool water, wildflowers, and a green meadow. Mountain bikers, runners, and dogs frequent this trail, especially after work and on weekends.

The trailhead is marked with a signpost and quickly turns northeast along the canyon. This gradual climb is sunny, warm, and dry in summer, and it may be a good idea

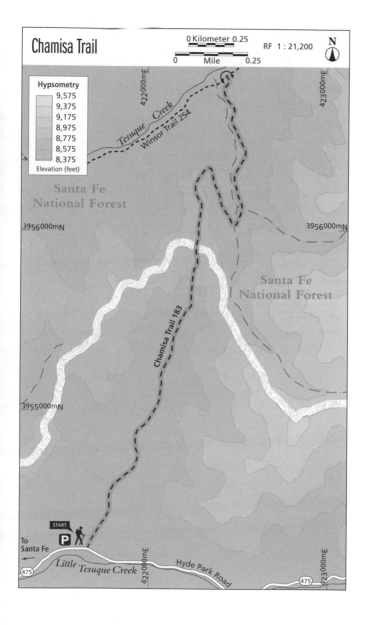

Chamisa Trail

0 Kilometer 0.25

0 Mile 0.25

RF 1 : 21,200

N

Hypsometry

9,575
9,375
9,175
8,975
8,775
8,575
8,375

Elevation (feet)

422000mE

423000mE

Tesuque Creek

Winsor Trail 254

Santa Fe
National Forest

3956000mN

3956000mN

Santa Fe
National Forest

Chamisa Trail 183

3955000mN

START

P

To
Santa Fe

475

Little Tesuque Creek

422000mE

Hyde Park Road

423000mE

475

to wait for a late-afternoon starting time. At about 1.5 miles from the trailhead, you will come to the top of a ridge, where there is a signpost and trail map. You may notice another trail to your left. This is an alternate route from the parking lot. Turn right (southeast) and follow the main trail downhill, descending into a canyon where the trail parallels a small stream. This portion of the hike is cool and shaded, and wildflowers thrive in early summer.

At 2.3 miles are two trail markers on wooden posts, indicating an intersection with Winsor Trail 254. This ends the Chamisa Trail, but to the immediate right is a pristine meadow providing pleasant resting places near the creek. Keep an eye out for the colorful western tanager, the Steller's jay who frequent the meadowlands, and Rocky Mountain flag (with wild iris).

Retrace your steps for your return hike, turning left (south) at the two posted signs near the meadow. When you reach the saddle be certain to go left (south) on the middle trail to return to the parking lot.

6 Borrego-Bear Wallow-Winsor Triangle

Type of hike: Loop.
Distance: 4 miles, round trip.
Elevation change: 750 feet.

Maps: Aspen Basin and McClure Reservoir (USGS), Pecos Wilderness (USFS).

Finding the trailhead: From Santa Fe Plaza drive north on Washington Avenue. Proceed through the intersection with Paseo de Peralta and turn right at the first light onto Artist's Road, which becomes Highway 475. Drive 8.5 miles to a parking lot on the left side of the road. Hyde Park RV Campground is on the left (west) about a quarter-mile before this turn, so be alert.

The Hike

This hike, which uses Borrego Trail (150), Bear Wallow Trail (182), and Winsor Trail (254), is wonderfully close to Santa Fe and is a quick getaway to the mountains and streams of the Sangre de Cristos. It is a beautiful fall hike, popular with runners, dogs, and bikers, so be prepared for all kinds of company, especially on weekends.

The trailhead, marked by the mileage post for Trails 182 and 254, is located at the far end of the parking lot. Douglas fir, Rocky Mountain maple, and large aspen line this wide, well-worn trail, which was once used to herd sheep to market from the north. The trail drops into a drainage, heading north, and after an easy 0.5 mile, turns left (northwest) at the junction of Borrego Trail 150 and Bear Wallow Trail 182. On your return you will loop back to this point on Borrego Trail. For the next mile you will follow Bear Wallow to the crossing of Big Tesuque Creek. Watch for changes in vegetation, especially on the southern slope, before you reach the

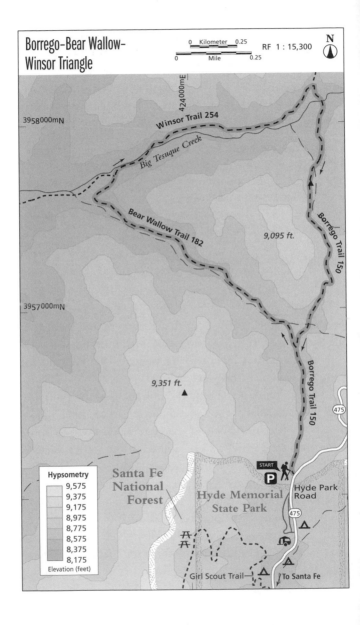

Borrego-Bear Wallow-Winsor Triangle

Kilometer 0 0.25   RF 1 : 15,300
Mile 0 0.25

N

Winsor Trail 254

424000mE

3958000mN

Big Tesuque Creek

Bear Wallow Trail 182

9,095 ft.

Borrego Trail 150

3957000mN

9,351 ft. ▲

Borrego Trail 150

475

Hypsometry

Elevation (feet)
9,575
9,375
9,175
8,975
8,775
8,575
8,375
8,175

Santa Fe National Forest

START
P

Hyde Memorial State Park

Hyde Park Road

475

Girl Scout Trail

To Santa Fe

stream crossing. We felt fortunate to find a tufted evening primrose just before starting the switchbacks leading to the creek. After crossing the creek you immediately intersect with Winsor Trail 254. This is a great place to rest, look for wild raspberries late in summer, and prepare for the uphill trek on your return. Take a right (east) onto Winsor Trail 254. Notice the charming miniature waterfalls as you walk steadily uphill, paralleling the creek.

At 2.5 miles you will encounter Borrego Trail 150 once again. Take a right (south) to begin the last leg of your hike. It takes but a minute and you once again cross a creek. A large, fallen ponderosa pine provides a bridge. The trail then ascends and descends on switchbacks. At 3.5 miles you will pass the Bear Wallow junction, which was your original route to the Big Tesuque Creek. Continue straight ahead on Borrego Trail, retracing your steps back to the trailhead.

7 Hyde Park Circle Trail

Type of hike: Loop.
Distance: 3.8 miles, round trip.
Elevation change: 1,000 feet.

Maps: Hyde Memorial State Park brochure available from New Mexico State Parks Division.

Finding the trailhead: From Santa Fe Plaza drive north on Washington Avenue. Proceed through the intersection with Paseo de Peralta and turn right at the first light onto Artist's Road, which becomes Highway 475. Drive approximately 7.4 miles until you reach the Hyde Memorial State Park Headquarters on the right (east). Park here and cross the street (west) to the trailhead. Circle Trail brochures are available in the kiosk across the creek.

The Hike

This hike is relatively short but quite steep, with about 1,000 feet of elevation gain in the first half of the hike. However, if you've done some previous hiking and are in a good state of fitness, the panoramic mountain and valley views are worth the effort.

Take the stone bridge over Little Tesuque Creek, and head left (south) up a rather steep set of switchbacks. We saw many small reptiles on this dry slope. The first section of this hike can be hot in the summer; be sure to take an adequate supply of water.

The trail has a good amount of shade, as aspen, Douglas fir, and ponderosa pine line the trail. The Hyde Park rangers have done a wonderful job maintaining this trail, and it is easy to follow steadily uphill for about 1.25 miles, where you reach the top of the ridge. Here you will find two picnic

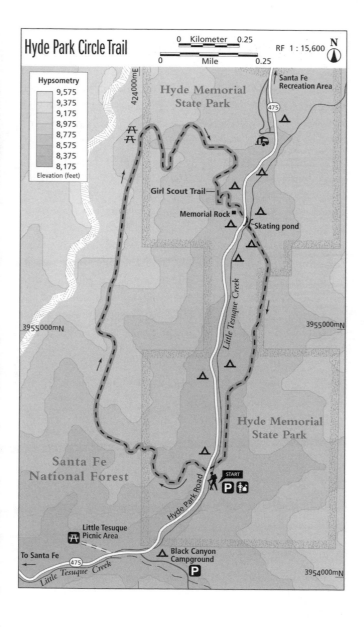

Hyde Park Circle Trail

0 Kilometer 0.25

0 Mile 0.25

RF 1 : 15,600

N

Hypsometry

9,575
9,375
9,175
8,975
8,775
8,575
8,375
8,175
Elevation (feet)

424000mE

Hyde Memorial
State Park

Santa Fe
Recreation Area

475

Girl Scout Trail

Memorial Rock

Skating pond

3955000mN

Little Tesuque Creek

3955000mN

Hyde Memorial
State Park

Santa Fe
National Forest

START

P

Hyde Park Road

Little Tesuque
Picnic Area

To Santa Fe

475

Little Tesuque Creek

Black Canyon
Campground

P

3954000mN

tables, welcome sights for a snack and water break. From this vantage point you can view the Sandia Mountains to the southwest and the Jemez Mountains to the northwest, across the Rio Grande valley. After resting follow the new sign indicating CIRCLE TRAIL to the right (east) and walk down a rather steep set of switchbacks to the bottom of the canyon. Be sure to stay on the main trail, as there are several points where the old trail is cordoned off by timbers.

When you can see the highway through the trees, the trail dead-ends with a junction. Go right, walk a short distance, and turn left (do not go uphill) onto part of the rock-lined Girl Scout Interpretive Nature Trail. At the time of updating, this trail was soon to be renovated, with new signs identifying the wildflowers and trees. Follow this trail, parallel to the road, going downhill (south). When you see a new wooden footbridge, across the highway just north of the skating pond, make your way in that direction. If you prefer to take the trail paralleling the highway back to the visitor center, it is approximately 1 mile downhill.

To continue the Circle Trail, cross the highway and the bridge and proceed left (north) up the hill for a short distance and then head south on the switchback. You will quickly come to the campground road. Cross this road and climb the set of stone stairs directly in front of you. There is the customary hiking trail sign at this point. Follow this trail, through the forest, across a footbridge, ascending and descending in a southward direction. You will see the campground shelters below to your right. Drainages and the thick pine needle cover often make it difficult to distinguish the trail, but if you lose it, merely hike to the campground road below and follow it to the visitor center. If you would like to find the trail again, it is easily located behind shelter #2.

From this point hike uphill and take the first trail to the right, leading to the bridge and creek crossing. It is an easy hike back to the trailhead from this point, as you gradually descend and traverse several drainages.

8 La Vega

Type of hike: Out-and-back.
Distance: 6.3 miles, round trip.
Elevation change: 890 feet.

Maps: Aspen Basin (USGS), Pecos Wilderness (SFNF).

Finding the trailhead: From Santa Fe Plaza drive north on Washington Avenue. Turn right at the first light after the intersection with Paseo de Peralta onto Artist's Road, which becomes Highway 475 and ends 14 miles from this point, at the Santa Fe Recreation Area. Park in the lower lot and walk north, toward Tesuque Creek, where you will see a large signpost for the Pecos Wilderness and also a marker for Winsor Trail 254.

The Hike

This trail begins at the Santa Fe Recreation Area (ski area), and has less use than those closer to Santa Fe. Its destination is a pristine meadow, complete with a stream running through it and a close-up view of Santa Fe Baldy. The maps of the area do not give the complete details of this hike; however, the trail is indicated by a trail marker and is easy to find.

Begin by crossing the bridge over Tesuque Creek and following Winsor Trail 254 to the right (east). In early summer marsh marigolds line the creek. As you ascend on fairly

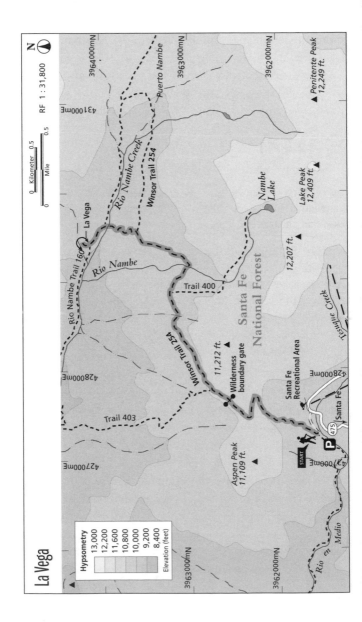

La Vega

Hypsometry

	Elevation (feet)
	13,000
	12,200
	11,600
	10,800
	10,000
	9,200
	8,400

N

RF 1 : 31,800

0 — Kilometer — 0.5

0 — Mile — 0.5

3964000mN

3963000mN

3962000mN

431000mE

Puerto Nambe

Rio Nambe Creek

Winsor Trail 254

Nambe Lake

Lake Peak 12,409 ft.

Penitente Peak 12,249 ft.

La Vega

Rio Nambe Trail 160

Rio Nambe

Trail 400

12,207 ft.

Santa Fe National Forest

428000mE

Winsor Trail 254

11,212 ft.

Wilderness boundary gate

Santa Fe Recreational Area

Tesuque Creek

427000mE

Trail 403

Aspen Peak 11,109 ft.

START

P

475

Santa Fe

410000mE

Rio en Medio

3963000mN

3962000mN

steep switchbacks for the next 0.5 mile, aspen and mixed conifer forests and meadows enclose you. The gate, indicating entrance to the Pecos Wilderness, is a welcome sight. If you stop to rest you may be visited by some resident gray jays looking for a handout.

The trail now descends for about a mile. You will pass a trail marker for Rio Nambe Trail 403 and another for Nambe Lake Trail 400; however, stay on Winsor Trail as it crosses Rio Nambe Creek and continues north. After about 2.5 miles you will see a sign on the right side of the trail for Upper Nambe Trail 101, Rio Nambe, and La Vega. Turn left (northeast) and start your descent into a beautiful grassy meadow with a large aspen stand.

You now descend to the lowest part of the hike, and cross Rio Nambe Creek. Head left (west), uphill, and come to the junction with Rio Nambe Trail 160 (about 2.8 miles into the hike). Go left (west) on Trail 160, which is rocky and narrow at this point. After a gradual descent and another ascent, you will find you have moved away from the creek. The trail turns northeast, up a hill through aspen trees to your destination. The sign indicating you have reached La Vega may or may not be standing, as vandals often consider these signs a treasure; however, if you walk a few yards ahead, you will find yourself in a vast meadow at the foot of Santa Fe Baldy. Enjoy exploring and resting. Begin your return trip at the signpost, follow Trail 160, cross the creek, and retrace your steps back to Trail 254, where you will turn right (west) to return to the Santa Fe Recreation Area.

9 Puerto Nambe Meadow

Type of hike: Out-and-back.
Distance: 9 miles, round trip.
Elevation change: 800 feet.

Maps: Aspen Basin (USGS), Pecos Wilderness (USFS).

Finding the trailhead: From Santa Fe Plaza drive north on Washington Avenue. At the first light after the intersection with Paseo de Peralta, turn right onto Artist's Road, which becomes Highway 475 and ends approximately 14 miles from this point, at the Santa Fe Recreation Area. Park in the lower lot and walk north, toward the creek, where you will see a large signpost for the Pecos Wilderness and a marker for Winsor Trail 254.

The Hike

This hike, along Winsor Trail 254, is quite demanding but well worth the time and energy necessary in order to obtain spectacular views of the peaks and valleys surrounding Santa Fe and an up-close experience of Santa Fe Baldy.

Begin by crossing the bridge at the marker for Winsor Trail 254 and turning right (east). In early summer white and yellow marsh marigolds line the creek. As you ascend on fairly steep switchbacks for the next 0.5 mile, lovely aspen and mixed conifer forests and gentle meadows surround you. The fence and gate, designating entrance to the Pecos Wilderness, are welcome sights, as this first ascent is now over! If you stop to rest you may be visited by some resident gray jays looking for a handout.

The trail now descends for about a mile. You will pass a marker for Rio Nambe Trail 403 and another for Nambe Lake Trail; however, stay on Winsor Trail as it crosses Rio

Puerto Nambe Meadow

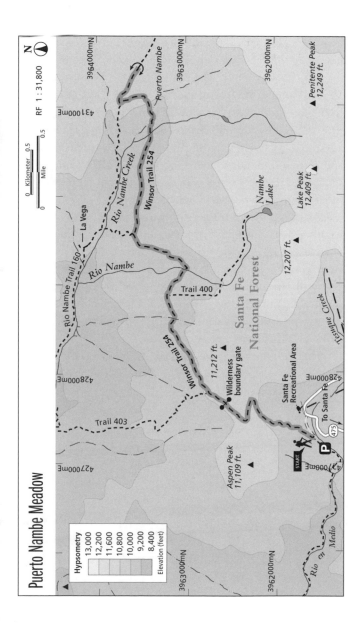

RF 1 : 31,800

Hypsometry

Elevation (feet)
- 13,000
- 12,200
- 11,600
- 10,800
- 10,000
- 9,200
- 8,400

Santa Fe National Forest

Rio Nambe Trail 160
La Vega
Rio Nambe Creek
Rio Nambe
Trail 400
Winsor Trail 254
Puerto Nambe
Trail 403
Aspen Peak 11,109 ft.
Winsor Trail 254
Wilderness boundary gate
11,212 ft.
12,207 ft.
Nambe Lake
Lake Peak 12,409 ft.
Penitente Peak 12,249 ft.
Santa Fe Recreational Area
START
To Santa Fe
475
Testuque Creek
Rio en Medio

0 Kilometer 0.5
0 Mile 0.5

Nambe and continues north. At about 2.5 miles into the hike, you will see a sign on the right side of the trail, pointing left, for Upper Nambe Trail 101, Rio Nambe, and La Vega. Continue straight ahead on Winsor Trail as it passes through a small grassy meadow. When you are once again in the conifer forest, a trail marker indicates Rio Nambe Trail 160 to your left. Remain on Winsor Trail. During late spring and early summer, this trail doubles as a small stream. It is a short hike through water and mud until you come to a set of challenging switchbacks, which leads you to the beautiful meadows and views of Puerto Nambe. As you walk into the meadow incredible vistas of Penitente Peak to the south, Lake Peak to the southwest, and Santa Fe Baldy to the north await you. The distant valley views are equal in grandeur. As you walk through the meadow, look for a trail marker that signifies the junction of Skyline and Winsor Trails and points the way to Lake Katherine (north). You might want to rest here and plan future hikes.

The trip home is quite painless—a reward for the uphill switchbacks you endured. Follow Winsor Trail back to the Santa Fe Recreation Area.

10 Tesuque Peak

Type of hike: Out-and-back.
Distance: 11.2 miles, round trip.
Elevation change: 1,855 feet.

Maps: Aspen Basin (USGS),
Pecos Wilderness (USFS).

Finding the trailhead: From Santa Fe Plaza drive north on Washington Avenue. Drive through the intersection with Paseo de Peralta and turn right at the first light onto Artist's Road, which becomes Highway 475. Follow the highway just past mile marker 13 to Aspen Vista picnic area, which is on the right side of the road. The trail starts after the gate at the upper (north) end of the picnic area parking lot.

The Hike

This hike is considered moderate in spite of the distance it covers. It follows Forest Road 150, a service road that accesses the radio and communication sites on Tesuque Peak, and has no steep inclines. We found that the wide, fairly even road makes it possible to hike side-by-side, which is a nice change from most mountain trails. Because of the elevation the weather can be unpredictable, so take along layers for every kind of weather. The high-elevation views afforded on this trail are spectacular, and it is, therefore, a very popular hike.

After walking through the Aspen Vista gate, you will be instantly surrounded by an aspen forest, one of the largest continuous stands in New Mexico. This is an ideal fall hike; however, when we hiked in early summer, wildflowers were abundant. Although there are three stream crossings over tributaries of Tesuque Creek, they are all covered by the road, so don't worry about wet feet on this long hike, unless

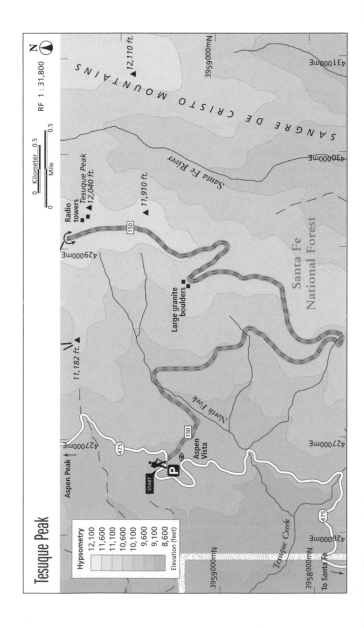

Tesuque Peak

Hypsometry

Elevation (feet)
12,100
11,600
11,100
10,600
10,100
9,600
9,100
8,600

RF 1 : 31,800

N

0   Kilometer   0.5
0   0.5
     Mile

SANGRE DE CRISTO MOUNTAINS

Radio towers
Tesuque Peak
▲ 12,040 ft.

▲ 12,110 ft.

▲ 11,910 ft.

Santa Fe River

150

Large granite boulders ■

Santa Fe National Forest

▲ 11,182 ft.

150

North Fork

Aspen Peak ←

475

START

P

Aspen Vista

Tesuque Creek

475

To Santa Fe

3959000mN

3958000mN

4260000mE
4270000mE
4280000mE
4290000mE
4300000mE
4310000mE

3959000mN

you hit snow near the top. At about 1.5 miles a look across the valley offers excellent long-distance views of Los Alamos and Black Mesa (a sacred site adjacent to San Ildefonso Pueblo).

Notice the vegetation change as you climb. The aspen forest gives way to subalpine evergreens and Engelmann spruce. About 2.5 miles into the hike there is a sharp, steep left turn and then the road levels out. We ran into some small snowfields in early June and started adding clothing to keep warm. At about 3.8 miles there is a clearing with a spectacular panoramic view of the valley. Walk a bit longer and you will find the perfect picnic spot amidst large granite boulders. From this point you can see your destination near the microwave towers of Tesuque Peak.

When you reach the ski area, you may simply turn around and retrace your steps back to the car, or if you wish a speedier descent, you can choose a ski run. If you decide upon the latter, head northwest down the slope to the right of the third snow fence. Use the green metal roof below as your guide to the bottom of the hill and the parking lot. This descent will take approximately one hour. From the parking lot we decided to hitchhike back to our car at Aspen Vista; however, during the week there were few cars, and we walked almost the entire 2-plus miles before getting a ride.

Pecos Wilderness

This 222,673-acre wilderness, most of which is located within the Santa Fe National Forest, lies 35 miles northeast of Santa Fe. Take Interstate 25 east from Santa Fe to the Glorieta exit and follow signs to the small town of Pecos. Here you may wish to make a side trip to the Pecos National Historical Park, where the ruins depict a thousand-year history of pueblo and Spanish mission life. From Pecos take Highway 63 north to the Pecos Wilderness. Within the boundaries of the wilderness lie many peaks over 13,000 feet, mountain lakes, and more than 150 miles of pristine streams. This area is heavily used by hikers and horses; therefore, consider getting out early on weekends, especially if you are planning to locate a campsite in one of the many highly accessible and well-maintained campgrounds. Motorized equipment and mechanized transportation, including mountain bikes, hunter carts, and chainsaws are prohibited in the Pecos Wilderness.

11 Glorieta Ghost Town Trail

Type of hike: Out-and-back.
Distance: 4.7 miles, round trip.
Elevation change: 600 feet.

Maps: Glorieta (USGS), McClure (USGS).

Finding the trailhead: From Santa Fe drive east on Interstate 25 toward Las Vegas, New Mexico. Take exit 299 to the Glorieta Conference Center. Turn left at the top of the ramp, cross the overpass, and turn left again. The gate for the conference center is 0.5 mile on your right. Identify yourself as a hiker to the caretaker, and follow the signs for "registration." You'll find a welcoming assistant on duty 24/7, with information regarding hiking from the center and the location of trailhead parking. Turn left from New Mexico Hall (registration) and follow Oak Street until you come to a storage building on the right. Park here and walk right onto the adjacent service road, heading northwest. Sign in on the hiker registry, located across from the staff RV parking lot, and continue through the gate and straight ahead.

The Hike

This is an easy hike, much of which is along a gentle stream, providing cool shade on hot summer days. It is a wonderful introduction to the diversity of the New Mexican landscape. The thought of a ghost town destination encourages you as you gently ascend through the forest.

At about 0.2 mile there is a sign indicating Glorieta Baldy and Broken Arrow Trail veering off to the left. Glorieta Ghost Town is straight ahead. At about 0.6 mile the road forks; stay on the larger trail to the right, the main road, and in a short distance you reach another gate. At approximately 1 mile the trail narrows and the aspens begin appearing.

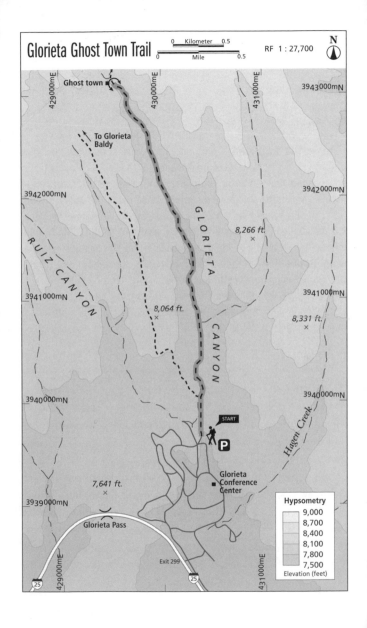

Glorieta Ghost Town Trail

Kilometer 0 0.5
Mile 0 0.5

RF 1 : 27,700

N

Ghost town ■

To Glorieta
Baldy

RUIZ CANYON

GLORIETA CANYON

8,266 ft. ×

8,064 ft. ×

8,331 ft. ×

Hagen Creek

START

P

Glorieta
Conference
Center

7,641 ft. ×

Glorieta Pass

Exit 299

25

25

429000mE
430000mE
431000mE
429000mE
431000mE

3943000mN
3942000mN
3941000mN
3940000mN
3939000mN
3942000mN
3941000mN
3940000mN

Hypsometry

9,000
8,700
8,400
8,100
7,800
7,500
Elevation (feet)

Shortly you'll see an old car mired in the streambed, reminding you of the past and what awaits you on the upper trail.

It is not long before you reach your destination. You will see a serene, open meadow, an old sawmill, and piles of timbers. You might be content to rest here, but just about 0.25 mile beyond this point is another wonderful meadow, in the midst of which sit remnants of an old hotel.

Rest and take in the beauty of the canyon surrounding you, and then retrace your steps back to the trailhead.

12 Cave Creek Trail

Type of hike: Out-and-back.
Distance: 3.6 miles, round trip.
Elevation change: 470 feet.

Maps: Cowles (USGS), Pecos Wilderness (USFS).

Finding the trailhead: From Santa Fe take Interstate 25 toward Las Vegas. Take exit 299 for Highway 50, Glorieta and Pecos. Follow Highway 50 to the town of Pecos and the intersection with Highway 63. Turn left onto Highway 63 and drive 20 miles to Cowles. In Cowles turn left over the bridge crossing the Pecos River, then turn at the first right onto the single-lane, paved Forest Road 305 to Panchuela campground (tent camping only). Go to the west end of the campground and find trail information on the bulletin board located beside the footbridge.

The Hike

This hike takes you to a set of caves along picturesque Cave Creek. It is appropriate as a family hike; however, the crossing of Panchuela Creek can be precarious during the spring and early summer runoff. This trail receives heavy use by hikers and horses.

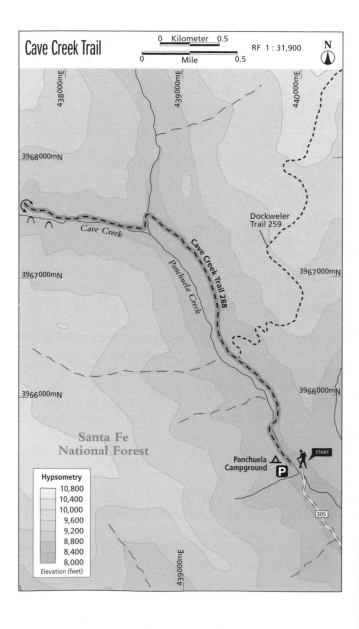

Cave Creek Trail

0 Kilometer 0.5

0 Mile 0.5

RF 1 : 31,900

N

438000mE

439000mE

440000mE

3968000mN

Cave Creek

Cave Creek Trail 288

Dockweler
Trail 259

Panchuela Creek

3967000mN

3967000mN

3966000mN

3966000mN

Santa Fe
National Forest

Panchuela
Campground

P

START

305

Hypsometry

| 10,800 |
| 10,400 |
| 10,000 |
| 9,600 |
| 9,200 |
| 8,800 |
| 8,400 |
| 8,000 |

Elevation (feet)

439000mE

After crossing the creek head upstream to the left (northwest) on Trail 288. The large, old Douglas firs along the trail are impressive, as are the wildflowers in early summer. As you hike, the trail parallels the creek, rises above it, and at about 0.8 mile comes to a junction with Dockweiler Trail 259, which forks to the right. Stay left (west) on Cave Creek Trail 288 as it winds through the valley. We met several people hiking out after a successful day of fishing.

At about 1.5 miles you will reach the confluence of Panchuela and Cave Creeks. Follow the trail to the left (west) over several logs, which make a rather precarious bridge. This is a beautiful spot to stop, rest, and examine the lush riparian vegetation.

The first set of caves lies about 0.4 mile up the trail on your left (south). A cairn and well-worn path mark the location. To find the second set of caves, look for a clearing and another path to the creek in less than 0.1 mile. You can cross the creek to examine the caves; however, the rocks are very slippery, and there are deep drop-offs inside the caves, so it is not safe to enter them.

After exploring return to the trailhead by retracing your route.

13 Beatty's Flats from Jack's Creek Campground

Type of hike: Out-and-back.
Distance: 15 miles, round trip.
Elevation change: 1,900 feet.

Maps: Elk Mountain (USGS), Pecos Falls (USGS), Cowles (USGS), Pecos Wilderness (USFS).

Finding the trailhead: From Santa Fe take Interstate 25 toward Las Vegas. Take exit 299 for Highway 50, Glorieta, and Pecos. Follow Highway 50 to the town of Pecos and the intersection with Highway 63. Turn left onto Highway 63 and drive through Terrero and Cowles. Jack's Creek Campground is 2.3 miles beyond Cowles on Highway 63. When you reach the campground, turn right into the wilderness parking and equestrian camping area. The trailhead for Trail 25 lies to the left (north) of the Pecos Wilderness map and information board. The fee for trailhead parking is $2.00.

The Hike

The destination for this hike is a large grassy meadow, the former location of an old mining cabin, built in the late 1800s. It is still referred to as Beatty's Cabin and is located near the confluence of the Pecos River and Rito del Padre. This area is often called the heart of the Pecos Wilderness because it is the junction for a large number of hiking trails.

The trailhead for Trail 25 is adjacent to equestrian facilities; therefore, it is a popular horse trail and can become extremely muddy in rainy weather.

The trail heads north with a gradual ascent among aspen, ponderosa pine, Gambel oak, and Douglas fir. It begins to gain greater elevation in a series of long switchbacks. On

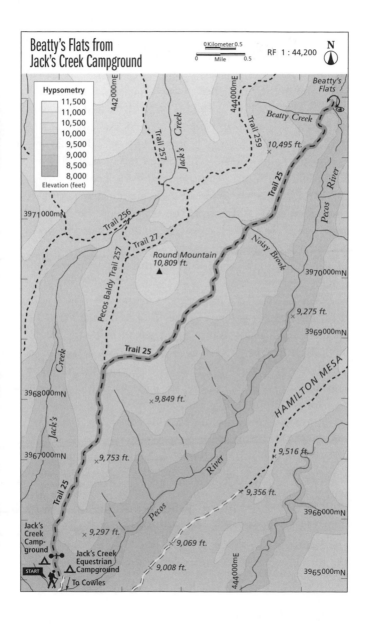

Beatty's Flats from
Jack's Creek Campground

0 Kilometer 0.5
0 Mile 0.5

RF 1 : 44,200

N

Hypsometry
11,500
11,000
10,500
10,000
9,500
9,000
8,500
8,000
Elevation (feet)

Beatty's Flats

Beatty Creek

442000mE

Jack's Creek

444000mE

Trail 259

Trail 257

10,495 ft.

Trail 25

Pecos River

3971000mN

Trail 256

Trail 27

Noisy Brook

3970000mN

Pecos Baldy Trail 257

Round Mountain
10,809 ft.

9,275 ft.

3969000mN

Trail 25

HAMILTON MESA

3968000mN

9,849 ft.

Jack's Creek

3967000mN

9,753 ft.

9,516 ft.

Pecos River

9,356 ft.

444000mE

3966000mN

Jack's
Creek
Camp-
ground

Trail 25

9,297 ft.

9,069 ft.

Jack's Creek
Equestrian
Campground

9,008 ft.

3965000mN

START

To Cowles

one of the last turns, a wooden fence and gate with an entrance for horses appear on the right; be certain to stay on the main trail, turning left (north). After the trail levels out at the top of the ridge, there is one more short climb before you are in a vast open meadow, dotted here and there with dark areas of aspens and mixed conifers. At approximately 2.5 miles a trail marker indicates that Beatty's Trail 25 proceeds straight (northeast) while Pecos Baldy Trail 257 turns to the left (northwest). Continue following Trail 25.

Although the trail gradually gains elevation as it skirts the east side of Round Mountain, this is a pleasant meadow hike with several small creek crossings. Wildflowers are plentiful, and there are large white and subalpine firs as well as groves of aspens along the trail, which you may be sharing with grazing cattle.

After leaving the meadow the trail makes a long, gradual descent to the Pecos River. There are several stream crossings and, true to its name, Noisy Brook seems to be the loudest and can be heard a good distance away. It is the largest of the streams, with a single log holding back the flow of water, creating a small, sandy pool. This is a fine resting spot and perhaps turnaround place, too.

If you continue, the trail quickly takes you to an open meadow with an excellent view of Hamilton Mesa to the right (east), before it descends through alternating conifer and aspen forests. Cow parsnip seems to be growing everywhere. Approximately 1.5 miles from Noisy Brook, a rock outcrop and large clearing appear to the right (east) of the trail. This is an overlook for the Pecos River Gorge and another place to either explore or rest. A wonderful view of the meadows at Beatty's Flats lies to the north, and should you choose to go on, there is one final descent to the flats area. Camping and fires are prohibited at Beatty's Flats.

Retrace your route for your return. When you are nearing the last leg of the hike, before leaving the meadow, you will find a most spectacular panoramic view of Santa Fe Baldy and Penitente Peaks to the southwest. You may also see elk in this area. A welcome descent takes you back to the trailhead.

14 Jack's Creek

Type of hike: Out-and-back.
Distance: 9 miles, round trip.
Elevation change: 2,100 feet.

Maps: Cowles (USGS), Truchas (USGS).

Finding the trailhead: From Santa Fe take Interstate 25 toward Las Vegas. Take exit 299 for Highway 50, Glorieta, and Pecos. Follow Highway 50 to the town of Pecos and the intersection with Highway 63. Turn left onto Highway 63 and drive through the communities of Terrero and Cowles. Jack's Creek Campground is 2.3 miles beyond Cowles on Highway 63. When you reach the campground, turn right into the wilderness parking and equestrian camping area. There is a $2.00 per day charge for parking. The trailhead for Trail 25 lies to the left (north) of the Pecos Wilderness map and information board.

The Hike

This is a hike filled with wonderful distant views of the high Pecos Wilderness peaks. Be sure to pack your camera in your backpack. If you decide to spend several days exploring this area, Jack's Creek Campground, the originating point of the

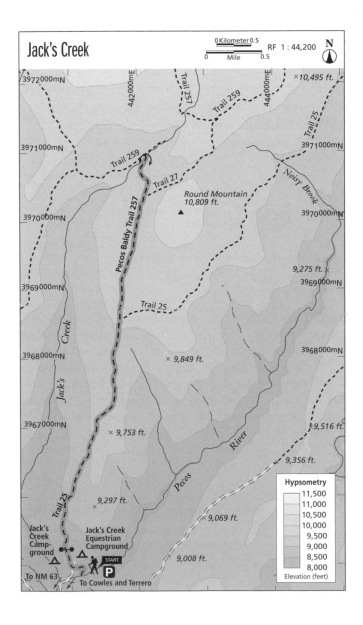

Jack's Creek

RF 1 : 44,200

N

| 0 Kilometer 0.5 |
| 0 Mile 0.5 |

Trail 257
Trail 259
Trail 25
×10,495 ft.
Trail 259
Trail 27
Round Mountain
10,809 ft.
▲
Noisy Brook
Pecos Baldy Trail 257
9,275 ft. ×
Trail 25
× 9,849 ft.
9,516 ft.
× 9,753 ft.
9,356 ft.
River
Pecos
× 9,297 ft.
× 9,069 ft.
Jack's Creek
Trail 25
9,008 ft.
Jack's Creek Campground
Jack's Creek Equestrian Campground
START
P
To NM 63
To Cowles and Terrero

442000mE
444000mE
3972000mN
3971000mN
3971000mN
3970000mN
3970000mN
3969000mN
3969000mN
3968000mN
3968000mN
3967000mN

Hypsometry	
	11,500
	11,000
	10,500
	10,000
	9,500
	9,000
	8,500
	8,000
Elevation (feet)	

hike, is located in a beautiful aspen meadow and is a great place to camp.

The trail heads north with a gradual ascent among aspen, ponderosa pine, Gambel oak, and Douglas fir before it begins to gain greater elevation in a series of long switchbacks. On one of the last turns, a wooden fence and gate for horses appear on the right; be certain to stay on the main trail, turning left (north). After the trail levels out at the top of the ridge, there is one more short climb before you are in a vast, open meadow dotted here and there with dark areas of aspens and mixed conifers.

At approximately 2.5 miles you will come to the junction of Trail 25, continuing east to Beatty's Flats, and Trail 257. Take 257 left (northwest) to Pecos Baldy Lake. You will find beautiful meadows with wild iris, aspen groves, and an occasional large Douglas fir surrounding the west side of Round Mountain. This is a great destination for a short day hike, as you already have wonderful views of Pecos Baldy ahead of you (northwest) and Redondo Peak and Santa Fe Baldy due west.

If you continue another 2 miles, you will hike past Round Mountain and reach Jack's Creek and the junction with Dockweiler Trail 259. This is a great resting spot and turnaround point. Retrace your route back to the trailhead.

Bandelier National Monument

D riving the 48 miles from Santa Fe to Bandelier offers a unique opportunity not only to view the geological features and breathtaking scenery of this corner of New Mexico, but to explore the nearby pueblos of Tesuque, Santa Clara, and San Ildefonso. Visiting San Ildefonso provides a close view of Black Mesa, the site of the 1692 reconquest of New Mexico by the Spanish forces. Be aware that it is held sacred by the Pueblo peoples and is closed to hiking.

Since the first nomadic peoples traveled here over 10,000 years ago, Bandelier has held a special place in New Mexico's history. The oral traditions and migration stories of many of the Pueblo people of New Mexico speak of the mesas and canyons of this area. From about A.D. 1150 to the mid-1500s, Frijoles Canyon was the home of the Ancestral Pueblo people, ancestors of the present-day Pueblo Indians. No one knows why they decided to leave, but they now inhabit nineteen different pueblos in New Mexico and speak five different languages.

In 1916 President Woodrow Wilson designated Bandelier a national monument. It has 32,000 acres of land, 90 percent of which is designated wilderness. Altitudes range from 5,330 feet at the Rio Grande to over 10,000 feet in the Jemez Mountains. There are more than 1,000 ruins within the 50 square miles of Bandelier, with a series of well-maintained trails leading to many of these ancient sites. Many of the (more than) 70 miles of hiking trails begin at the Bandelier Visitor Center and focus on the Frijoles Canyon cliff dwellings nearby. There is some wheelchair accessibility on these hikes. Be sure to visit the headquarters museum and bookstore and also the gift shop, which offers art of the nearby pueblos.

A wonderful campground lies close to the entrance of Bandelier, and when attempting to make reservations, we were told it was not necessary, as it has never been filled to capacity.

Bandelier's main area closes at dusk, so plan your hikes accordingly. Be sure to prepare for hot summer hiking by carrying enough water, sunscreen, and a hat!

15 Burnt Mesa Trail

Type of hike: Out-and-back.
Distance: 5 miles.
Elevation change: 300 feet.

Maps: Bandelier National Monument (Trails Illustrated Topo Map), Frijoles (USGS).

Finding the trailhead: From Santa Fe drive north on U.S. Highways 84/285. In Pojoaque follow signs for Los Alamos and Highway 502 for approximately 12 miles to the junction with Highway 4. Take Highway 4 south, passing the entrance to Bandelier National Monument. Drive for another 3.9 miles past the entrance and turn into the trailhead parking area on the left side of the road.

The Hike

This is an easy, level hike with panoramic views of the neighboring mesas. Burnt Mesa was in the midst of the La Mesa Fire of 1977 and much of the landscape remains open. There are a number of ruins located along this trail. They are thought to have been inhabited between A.D. 1150 and A.D. 1600, although there has been little archaeological work done on the mesa.

Note the bulletin board at the trailhead with information regarding the fire and the vegetation in this area. Walk south on the trail and very shortly the trail branches. Take the left fork. The landscape is filled with juniper, oak, and small ponderosa pine. At about 1 mile the first mound of archaeological rubble can be seen to the right of the trail. The second mound is at about 2 miles on the left, and there are two additional, at 2.5 and 3 miles. Remember that collecting archaeological or historic artifacts or disturbing archaeological sites is a felony offense.

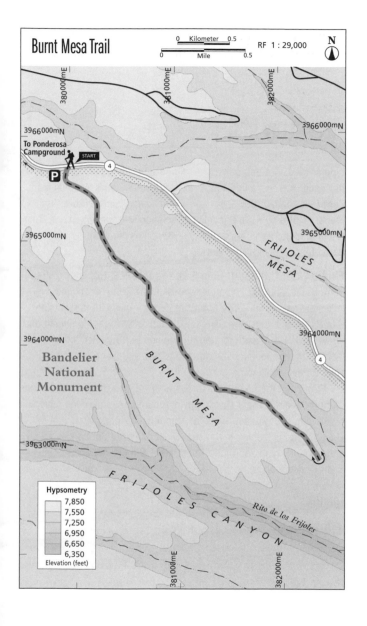

Burnt Mesa Trail

0 —— Kilometer —— 0.5

0 —— Mile —— 0.5

RF 1 : 29,000

N

380000mE

381000mE

382000mE

3966000mN

3966000mN

To Ponderosa
Campground

START

4

P

3965000mN

3965000mN

FRIJOLES

MESA

3964000mN

3964000mN

**Bandelier
National
Monument**

BURNT

MESA

4

3963000mN

3963000mN

FRIJOLES CANYON

Rito de los Frijoles

Hypsometry

	Elevation (feet)
	7,850
	7,550
	7,250
	6,950
	6,650
	6,350

381000mE

382000mE

Walk to the end of the mesa and enjoy the views of the surrounding canyons before turning around and retracing your route back to the trailhead.

16 Frey Trail

Type of hike: Out-and-back.
Distance: 4 miles, round trip.
Elevation change: 600 feet.
Maps: Frijoles (USGS), Bandelier National Monument (Trails Illustrated Topo Maps), Hiking Trails and Jeep Roads of Los Alamos County, Bandelier National Monument and Vicinity (Otowi Station Science Museum Shop and Book Store, Los Alamos).

Finding the trailhead: From Santa Fe take U.S. Highways 285/84 north to Pojoaque. At Pojoaque take Highway 502 (west), following signs for Los Alamos. Drive approximately 12 miles, to the junction with Highway 4, following signs for Bandelier National Monument and White Rock. Drive south for about 25 miles to Bandelier. Turn left (south) into the monument entrance, where you pay a fee of $10, good for the whole week.

Follow the road a short distance until you see the sign for Juniper Campground. Turn right (west), driving past the campground registration booth, until you see signs for amphitheater parking on your left. The trailhead is located in the southwest corner of the parking lot and is clearly marked. Tyuonyi Ruins are 1.6 miles from this point, and the visitor center is 2 miles.

The Hike

The Frey Trail, once called the Old North Trail, was used by all visitors to Bandelier until 1934, when the Civilian Conservation Corps built the present road. For ten years it was the only trail Mrs. Evelyn Frey, for whom the trail was

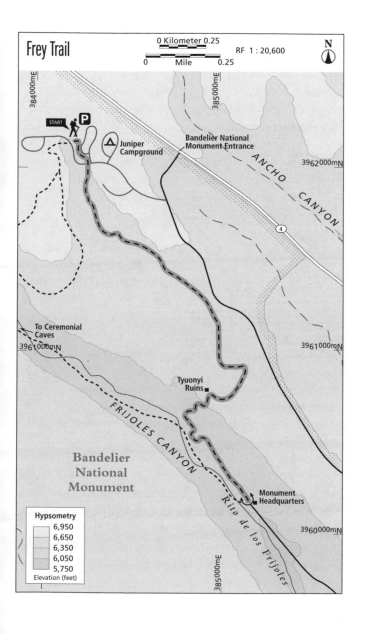

Frey Trail

0 Kilometer 0.25   RF 1 : 20,600

0 Mile 0.25

N

384000mE

START **P**

Juniper Campground

385000mE

Bandelier National Monument Entrance

ANCHO CANYON

3962000mN

4

To Ceremonial Caves

3961000mN

Tyuonyi Ruins

FRIJOLES CANYON

Bandelier National Monument

Monument Headquarters

Rito de los Frijoles

3961000mN

3960000mN

385000mE

Hypsometry

Elevation (feet)
6,950
6,650
6,350
6,050
5,750

named, and her husband used as access to their home and guest lodge in Frijoles Canyon.

The hike provides an excellent opportunity to obtain an overview of Frijoles Canyon and Tyuonyi Ruins before setting out to explore them in depth. The trail descends to the park headquarters, where you may enjoy visiting the museum, bookstore, or gift shop before hiking back to your car.

Because of the steep drop-offs, be careful with children. Also, be certain to take water with you, do not bring pets or bikes, and remember that the monument closes at dusk.

The trail begins by heading southeast from the amphitheater parking lot. A short distance into the hike you will cross a paved road. Soon you will cross a second road and head east (left). It is well marked. Along the trail you will see evidence of the elk that inhabit this area, and you will also see much evidence of the fire of 2000, along with the dramatic effects of drought and beetle infestation on the plateau vegetation. At 1 mile you have reached the rim of the canyon, and there is a spectacular view of the canyon and the ruins to the east. This is a good turnaround point if you are not up to the steep descent or the taxing ascent of your return route.

A series of switchbacks takes you to the bottom of the canyon. When you come to the first fork in the trail, take a right and at the next fork a left, following the sign to the visitor center. You will walk through the Tyuonyi Ruins but may want to return with the self-guided pamphlet, which is available at the center. In addition to exploring these ruins, you may wish to visit the Ceremonial Cave, with its restored kiva, an easy 1.4-mile hike up Frijoles Canyon. Be sure to save some energy for the 600-foot ascent back to the trailhead.

17 Frijoles Canyon Trail (Ponderosa Campground to Bandelier Park Headquarters)

Type of hike: One-way (shuttle required).

Distance: 7.5 miles.

Elevation change: 550 feet.

Maps: Frijoles (USGS), Bandelier National Monument (Trails Illustrated Topo Maps), Hiking Trails and Jeep Roads of Los Alamos County, Bandelier National Monument and Vicinity (Otowi Station Science Museum Shop and Book Store, Los Alamos).

Finding the trailhead: The starting point for this hike is Ponderosa Campground, located on Highway 4, 6 miles west of the Bandelier National Monument entrance. From Santa Fe take U.S. Highways 285/84 north to Pojoaque. At Pojoaque take Highway 502 west, following the signs for Los Alamos. Follow Highway 502 for approximately 12 miles to the junction with Highway 4. Take Highway 4 (south), following signs for Bandelier National Monument and White Rock. In approximately 25 miles (from Highway 502) you will pass the entrance for Bandelier National Monument. Continue for 6 miles to Ponderosa Campground, on the left side of the highway. Turn here and make your way to the parking area. Follow the sign for Frijoles Canyon/Upper Crossing. An alternate plan is to enter Bandelier National Monument, park your car at the monument headquarters, and arrange a shuttle to Ponderosa Campground.

The Hike

Although this hike necessitates a shuttle or a ride back to the trailhead, it provides exposure to the wonders of Frijoles Canyon. It is worth the effort to arrange a ride, either

Frijoles Canyon Trail (Ponderosa Campground to Bandelier Park Headquarters)

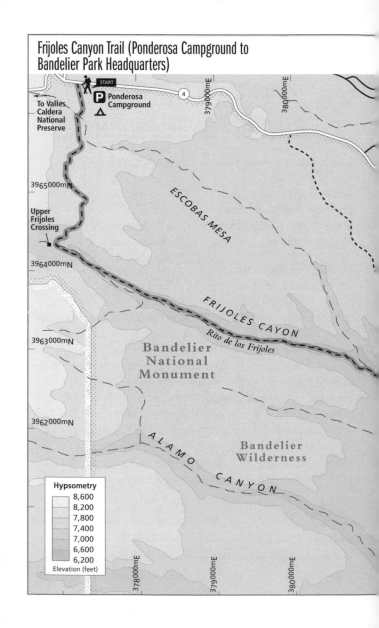

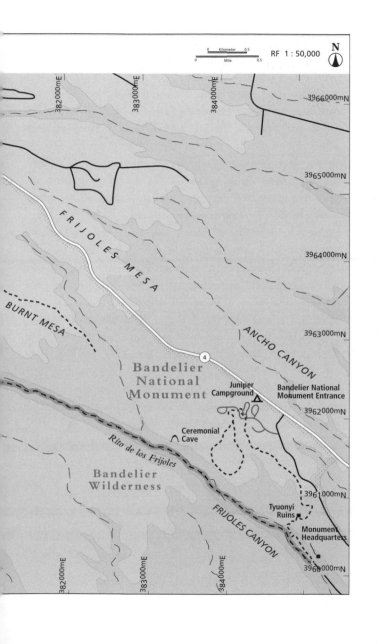

at the beginning of the hike or the end. The Rito de los Frijoles is a permanent stream in the bottom of the canyon, which nourishes the incredible riparian diversity you will see, and sustains many canyon animals and birds. It's a cool getaway in summer. Beware of poison ivy along the trail.

The early part of the hike is easy and level as you walk along a fire road to the canyon edge. Here the trail takes you down a long series of switchbacks to the bottom of Frijoles Canyon, Upper Crossing, and Rito de los Frijoles (Little River of the Beans). Cross the creek and turn left, following the trail marker for Frijoles Canyon Trail and the visitor center. The hike parallels the stream, and we were happy to have our hiking poles for the numerous high water crossings in early April. There are gentle ascents and descents through two camping zones (reservations required). Along with the diversity of vegetation, there are boulders and high vertical tuff cliffs, creating very interesting and narrow passageways.

Approximately 1.4 miles before the visitor center, the Ceremonial Cave appears to your left, 150 feet above the trail. The cave was occupied from approximately A.D. 1250 to A.D. 1600. It is thought that it was not ceremonial at all, but rather a protected habitation site with a small kiva. It is definitely worth the climb up the series of ladders.

The remainder of the hike is on an easy and heavily used trail back to the monument headquarters.

18 Falls Trail

Type of hike: Out-and-back.
Distance: 5 miles, round trip.
Elevation change: 700 feet.
Maps: Frijoles (USGS), Bandelier National Monument (Trails Illustrated Topo Maps), Hiking Trails and Jeep Roads of Los Alamos County, Bandelier National Monument and Vicinity (Otowi Station Science Museum Shop and Book Store, Los Alamos).

Finding the trailhead: From Santa Fe take U.S. Highways 285/84 north to Pojoaque. At Pojoaque take Highway 502 west, following signs to Los Alamos, for approximately 12 miles, to the junction with Highway 4. Take Highway 4 south to Bandelier National Monument, approximately 25 miles from the junction of Highway 502. Turn left into the monument entrance, where you pay a fee of $10, which is good for the whole week. Follow the road for about 3 miles to park headquarters, cross the bridge at the end of the parking lot, turn left, and look for designated backcountry parking. The trailhead is at the far (south) end of the parking lot.

The Hike

This hike provides an opportunity to see not only the natural beauty of the falls but also the geologic history and vegetative diversity present in Frijoles Canyon. You will pass two waterfalls on your way to the Rio Grande. The hike begins close to the monument bookstore and museum, giving you the opportunity to pick up the self-guide pamphlet, "A Guide to Falls Trail, Bandelier National Monument." It is an excellent source for detailed information on the geology of the entire Jemez Mountain area. When planning this hike keep in mind that the monument closes at dusk.

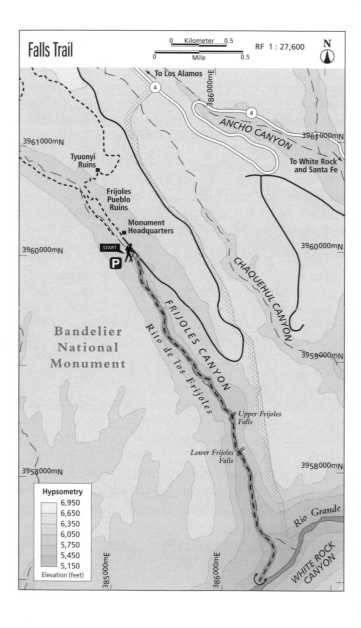

A marker at the trailhead indicates that Upper Falls is 1.5 miles, Lower Falls is 2 miles, and the Rio Grande is 2.5 miles (elevation change of 700 feet). The wide, well-maintained and well-used path winds along, near, and beside El Rito de los Frijoles (Little River of the Beans) and through a juniper and large ponderosa pine forest.

After approximately a mile you will begin your descent into the canyon. Bordering the trail are tent rocks, eroded columns of volcanic rock (tuff) that were escape routes for hot gases millions of years ago. Also notice the tuff cliffs above you as you approach the stream. Several sturdy wooden bridges in this area make creek crossings easy, and the vegetation is wonderfully varied as you walk closer to the falls. Our most interesting find for the day was the large banana yucca.

The overlook at the falls affords you a view not only of the waterfall, but also of the canyon's unique geology. You will now enter the bottom of the canyon; the stream that was next to you is now far below. Look back to see the second falls behind you.

As you continue on the trail to the Rio Grande, you will encounter many stream crossings. The last portion of the trail takes you into a treeless, wide-open area that is the result of unusually high runoff and flooding from the Cochiti Dam in 1985. The abundance of dead juniper provides an excellent habitat for many birds, including swallows and mountain bluebirds. You may notice canyon grape, another unusual plant. The sandy beach at the edge of the Rio Grande is a great place to relax before retracing your route uphill to the trailhead.

19 Apache Springs to Ponderosa Campground

Type of hike: Loop (requires a shuttle).
Distance: 7.5 miles, round trip.
Elevation change: 1,150 feet.
Maps: Frijoles (USGS), Bandelier National Monument (Trails Illus-trated Topo Maps), Hiking Trails and Jeep Roads of Los Alamos County, Bandelier National Monument and Vicinity (Otowi Station Science Museum Shop and Book Store, Los Alamos).

Finding the trailhead: From Santa Fe drive north on U.S. Highways 285/84 north to Pojoaque. At Pojoaque take Highway 502 west, following signs for Los Alamos. Follow Highway 502 for approximately 12 miles to the intersection of Highway 4. Drive south on Highway 4, following signs for White Rock and Bandelier National Monument, for about 32.2 miles. En route you will pass the Bandelier entrance at approximately 25 miles from the junction with Highway 502. The trailhead is 7.2 miles beyond this entrance. You will then pass the junction with Highway 501 and the old "back gate" still intact from the years when Los Alamos was a closed city. Continue straight ahead on Highway 4. The trailhead can be identified by a small parking lot and a gate numbered 10 on the left (south) side of the road between mile markers 48 and 49. You will also find an information board for Bandelier backcountry hiking.

The Hike

This hike takes you into the Bandelier Wilderness to experience quite a different environment from the summer crowds and activity centering around Bandelier Park Headquarters.

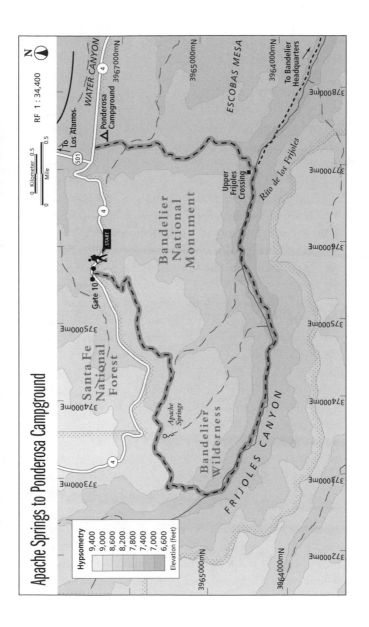

Apache Springs to Ponderosa Campground

Hypsometry

9,400
9,000
8,600
8,200
7,800
7,400
7,000
6,600

Elevation (feet)

RF 1 : 34,400

0   Kilometer   0.5

0   0.5
Mile

N

Santa Fe National Forest

Apache Springs

Bandelier Wilderness

FRIJOLES CANYON

Gate 10

START

To Los Alamos

WATER CANYON

501

4

Ponderosa Campground

Bandelier National Monument

Upper Frijoles Crossing

Rito de los Frijoles

ESCOBAS MESA

To Bandelier Headquarters

3967000mN

3965000mN

3964000mN

3965000mN

3964000mN

373000mE
374000mE
375000mE
376000mE
377000mE
378000mE
373000mE
372000mE

We found steep descents and ascents, rare wildflowers, and welcoming Frijoles Creek—all in all a great day hike!

From the trailhead an old logging road takes you south through a forest of Gambel oak, ponderosa pine, aspen, and evidence of the 2000 wildfire. Among the wildflowers in bloom along the trail in July were beautiful bright red sky-rocket penstamen. The trail quickly cuts through a meadow and gently ascends a ridge where, at about 0.4 miles, you will find a sign for Apache Springs pointing right (southwest). The next portion of the hike cuts through the La Mesa burn of 1977. New Mexican locust and aspen line the trail.

At about 1.2 miles you will come to the rim of a canyon and the Bandelier Wilderness boundary. Descend to the right (southwest) into the canyon. At the bottom a sign signals Apache Springs to your left (east). The actual spring is just a short distance from this point and is encased in concrete and stone. It was once used as a watering hole for cows and sheep on their way to summer pasture from the Espanola Valley to the Valle Grande (Valles Caldera National Preserve).

To continue return to the sign and follow the trail west, as it climbs up and out of the canyon. Be sure to stay on the main trail, and at about 2.5 miles you will reach the rim of Frijoles Canyon. The trail leads to the right (southwest), and you descend 800 feet to the canyon bottom on rocky, steep switchbacks. Unusual volcanic rock formations can be seen across the canyon, to the south. Frijoles Creek awaits you at the end of this difficult (and potentially hot) 0.5-mile descent. After an easy crossing on rocks the trail heads left (east), paralleling the creek. In late July this was a hot and humid but level part of the hike. We felt fortunate to find the endangered Rocky Mountain Lily in bloom;

however, we also found stinging nettles and poison ivy, so beware.

After walking a little over 3 miles on the canyon floor, a trail marker points the way to Ponderosa Campground (your destination), approximately 1.5 miles and a 450-foot climb. Follow the trail across a footbridge to the left (north) and up a series of switchbacks (we counted 13). The trail gradually works its way through a ponderosa forest, the campground, and to Highway 4. Walk 1.7 miles on the highway (unfortunately uphill) back to the trailhead and your car.

Los Alamos

Hiking in this area of northern New Mexico is more remote and less populated with hikers than the trails closer to Santa Fe, and a trip into the once secret city of Los Alamos is highly encouraged. The Bradbury Science Museum located on Central Avenue in Los Alamos offers a detailed history of the Manhattan Project as well as many hands-on exhibits that explain the current work of the Los Alamos National Laboratory. The short film depicting the founding of this unique city is especially interesting and informative.

A short drive west on Central Avenue brings you to the Fuller Lodge Complex. This beautiful log structure was the center of activity for the historic boarding school, which later became the focal point of the Atomic City. Here you will also find the Los Alamos Historical Museum and Book Shop, offering a wonderful miniview of the history of the Pajarito Plateau as well as other exhibits and memorabilia from the early days of Los Alamos. A drive around Los Alamos, with its interconnecting plateaus and varied forms of construction, reveals the history of a city built quickly and in secrecy.

As in Santa Fe, Los Alamos has recently developed a network of urban trails. Information on these hikes can be obtained from the Los Alamos Chamber of Commerce, 109 Central Park Square. Ask for a Los Alamos County trail network map.

The White Rock Tourist Information Center on Highway 4, White Rock, also has a very informative hiking pamphlet entitled, "50 Hikes in the Los Alamos Area."

Be aware that many canyon and mesa areas belonging to LANL (Los Alamos National Laboratory) are closed to trespassing and are marked accordingly.

20 Ancho Rapids

Type of hike: Out-and-back.
Distance: 6.5 miles, round trip.
Elevation change: 900 feet.
Maps: White Rock (USGS) (trail not identified), Santa Fe National Forest (USFS) (trail not identified), Hiking Trails and Jeep Roads of Los Alamos County, Bandelier National Monument and Vicinity (Otowi Station Science Museum Shop and Book Store, Los Alamos) (trail not identified).

Finding the trailhead: From Santa Fe take U.S. Highways 285/84 north to Pojoaque. At Pojoaque take Highway 502 west, following signs for Los Alamos, for approximately 12 miles, until you reach the intersection with Highway 4. Follow Highway 4 south into White Rock. After the first traffic light, the visitor center can be seen on the right. Set your odometer at this point. You will come to the trailhead in 3.9 miles. As you drive along Highway 4 notice the gates on the left side of the highway, giving access to the canyons. When leaving White Rock the gate numbers become smaller. You are looking for gate 4 (the trailhead) and the small gravel parking area in front of it. It is very near mile marker 60.

The Hike

This is a desert plateau and canyon hike to the Rio Grande River. After an easy beginning on high desert terrain, the trail descends along switchbacks, through a small, lush riparian area, and it ends on the sandy banks and smooth black boulders bordering the Rio Grande. There is no shade on this hike, and in the heat of summer it could be a scorcher, so it may be a good idea to wait for a cool day.

The trail begins on a very flat dirt road, constructed for the powerlines under which you will walk. Notice the wonderful views of the Rio Grande Valley, Sangre de Cristo

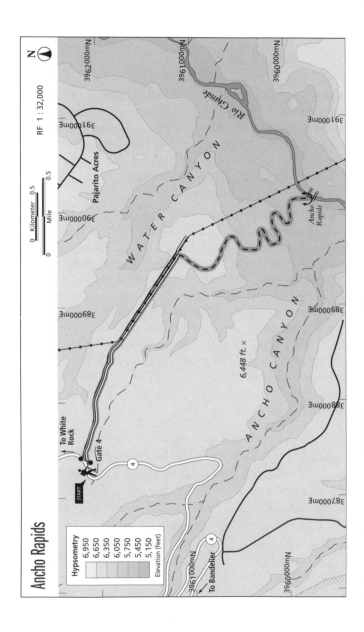

Ancho Rapids

Hypsometry

Elevation (feet)

- 6,950
- 6,650
- 6,350
- 6,050
- 5,750
- 5,450
- 5,150

RF 1 : 32,000

N

0   Kilometer   0.5

0   Mile   0.5

Pajarito Acres

WATER CANYON

Rio Grande

3962000mN

3961000mN

3960000mN

391000mE

390000mE

389000mE

388000mE

387000mE

3961000mN

3960000mN

To White Rock

Gate 4

START

4

To Bandelier

4

ANCHO CANYON

6,448 ft. ×

Ancho Rapids

Mountains, and the Sandia Mountains near Albuquerque (beyond the big white satellite dish belonging to Los Alamos National Laboratory). If hiking in early summer, you may want to get some close-up photographs of the bright yellow prickly pear cacti that flourish in the desert sand.

Continue walking on the road adjacent to the powerline towers, and at 1.6 miles (between the fifth and sixth towers) the road veers to your right (southeast). After about 0.25 mile this road ends. Walk to the left (south) up a slight incline, and then look to your right to find a cairn leading to an old fence and gate, which guard the rim of Ancho Canyon. Walk to the right (southeast) of the fence and follow the path through the pink sandstone cliffs, where you begin your descent into the canyon.

The expansive view from the boulders on the edge of the canyon shows you the trail below, which meanders through the dry canyon, through a lush riparian area, and eventually to the river. A long series of switchbacks, with more great photo opportunities, brings you to the bottom of the canyon. In early summer the cholla cacti are in bloom along this descent. Again, look for the cairns to guide you along the path on the canyon bottom; the vegetation changes and becomes more varied as you approach a spring. Follow the spring south to the Rio Grande. The rewards are great—a wonderful sandy beach with beautiful black boulders and Ancho Rapids roaring before you.

The only damper on your relaxation may be the anticipation of the hike back. You can easily locate the return trail by looking back up the canyon to your starting place, which is marked with a big splash of white, at the edge of the cliffs. This marks your path as you retrace your steps up the canyon and then hike back to gate 4 and your car.

21 Guaje Trail

Type of hike: Out-and-back.
Distance: 5.6 miles, one way.
Elevation change: 400 feet.
Maps: Valle Toledo (USGS), Hiking Trails and Jeep Roads of Los Alamos County, Bandelier National Monument and Vicinity (Otowi Station Science Museum Shop and Book Store, Los Alamos), Santa Fe National Forest (USFS).

Finding the trailhead: From Santa Fe take U.S. Highways 285/84 north to Pojoaque. At Pojoaque take Highway 502 west, following signs for Los Alamos, approximately 12 miles, to the junction with Highway 4. Take Highway 4 west, following the signs for White Rock and Bandelier. At 1.4 miles take Highway 501 right (north) on East Jemez Road (the truck route) to Los Alamos. When you enter the city, you will see the Los Alamos National Laboratory to your left. Go straight through the intersection with Diamond Drive, and approximately 1.5 miles from this intersection look for the sign for Pajarito Mountain Ski Area to your right (east). Turn and drive for approximately 4 miles to the ski hill. Park at the far (west) end of the parking lot and walk a short distance to a dirt road on the right (north) where you will see a trail marker for Guaje Canyon Trail 282.

The Hike

This hike is called the Quemazon Trail on the Hiking Trails and Jeep Roads of Los Alamos County map. It begins north of Los Alamos at the Pajarito Ski Area and gives an easy introduction to the gentle and inviting Jemez Mountains. In addition, the beautiful meadow Canada Bonita lies directly in your path. The route from Santa Fe takes you to the city of Los Alamos, where you may want to spend time learning the history of this once secret city.

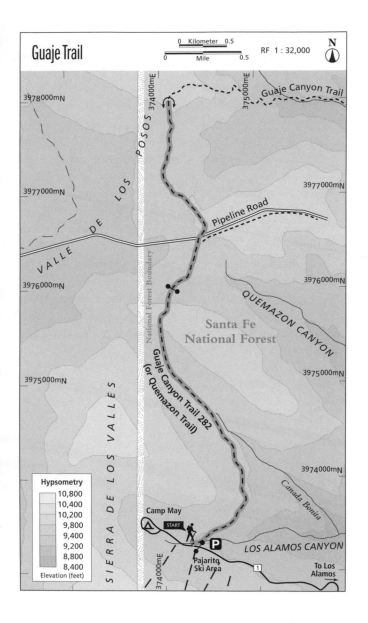

Guaje Trail

0 Kilometer 0.5
0 Mile 0.5

RF 1 : 32,000

N

Guaje Canyon Trail

3978000mN

374000mE

375000mE

3977000mN

VALLE DE LOS POSOS

Pipeline Road

National Forest Boundary

3976000mN

QUEMAZON CANYON

Santa Fe
National Forest

3975000mN

Guaje Canyon Trail 282
(or Quemazon Trail)

SIERRA DE LOS VALLES

3977000mN

3976000mN

3975000mN

3974000mN

Cañada Bonita

Hypsometry

10,800	
10,400	
10,200	
9,800	
9,400	
9,200	
8,800	
8,400	

Elevation (feet)

Camp May

START

Pajarito
Ski Area

P

LOS ALAMOS CANYON

1

To Los
Alamos

374000mE

Guaje trail heads northeast on the dirt road, and you are immediately confronted with a metal gate. You will then pass a cross-country ski trail angling off to the left; stay on the main trail. At approximately 1 mile you will come to a large meadow called Canada Bonita (pretty watercourse), which is a USDA Forest Service Research Natural Area, protected because of its unique montane grassland. The trail skirts the south end of the meadow and then turns north, where there is a wonderful view of the Rio Grande Valley to the southeast. As you ascend through aspen trees, the trail reaches its highest elevation of 9,570 feet, and the conifer forest begins.

Continue walking through a second metal gate. In about 0.5 mile you will see Pipeline Road to the right. Walk straight ahead, uphill, to a sign marking Guaje Canyon Trail to the left (northwest). This is your turnaround point, or you may wish to follow Guaje Canyon Trail for a short time, as it offers beautiful vistas of the valley to your left (west). Simply retrace your steps in order to return to the trailhead and the ski area.

22 Quemazon Trail

Type of hike: Out-and-back.
Distance: 6.2 miles, round trip.

Elevation change: 1,400 feet.
Map: Quaje Mountains (USGS).

Finding the trailhead: From Santa Fe drive north on U.S. Highways 84/285. In Pojoaque follow signs for Los Alamos and Highway 502. Drive through Los Alamos, taking Trinity Drive to the intersection with Diamond Drive. Cross this intersection, staying on Trinity Drive as it winds through a residential area for 0.6 mile. At this point turn left (the street names and numbers become confusing as you drive this loop, so merely take your first left after Forty-seventh Street). Take an immediate left onto the water tank access road, where trailhead parking is available.

The Hike

This hike is well-known for the numerous wagon wheel tracks etched into the volcanic rock, evidence that this historic trail was once the wagon road between the Espanola Valley and the Valle Grande (Valles Caldera National Preserve). It makes a good cold-weather hike, as there is little chance of mud on this volcanic rock road. The Cerro Grande fire of 2000 was devastating to this area; however, the forests are resilient and natural restoration is everywhere. The vistas of the Rio Grande Valley and also the Pajarito Ski Area are excellent, and you may also see a herd of elk. You will undoubtedly meet bikers, who frequent this trail.

Begin at the water tower and walk northwest to the second water tower. Turn left (west) and almost immediately you will see a small trail to your left (west). This is a mile-long nature trail (287A), which local elementary schoolchildren

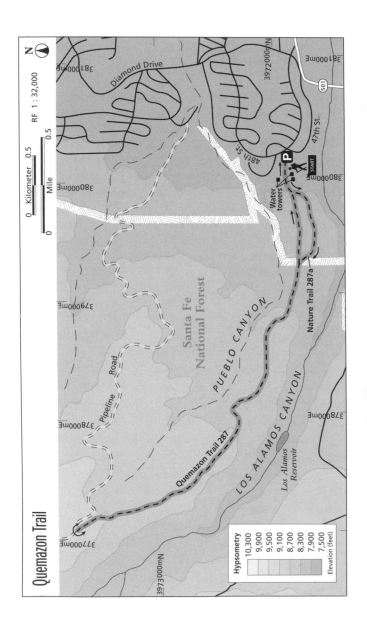

Quemazon Trail

0 Kilometer 0.5

RF 1 : 32,000

0 Mile 0.5

N

Diamond Drive

Santa Fe National Forest

PUEBLO CANYON

LOS ALAMOS CANYON

Pipeline Road

Quemazon Trail 287

Nature Trail 287a

Los Alamos Reservoir

Water towers

48th St.

47th St.

501

P

START

3810000mE

3800000mE

3790000mE

3780000mE

3777000mE

3972000mN

3973000mN

Hypsometry	
10,300	
9,900	
9,500	
9,100	
8,700	
8,300	
7,900	
7,500	
Elevation (feet)	

are using as a fire study area. It is easy to follow, lined with rocks in many places, and is a gentler ascent than the Quemazon Trail.

At the point where the nature trail rejoins the Quemazon Trail, the wagon ruts are very pronounced. It is a long, constant ascent for the remainder of the hike; however, it is not steep. It is very interesting to observe the forest regeneration. The sun-loving species, predominantly aspen, are among the first to appear after wildfire. Once established, the new aspen forest provides shade and a cooler ground temperature, allowing the shade-loving fir and spruce to flourish.

After approximately 3 miles the Douglas fir forest, which remained unscathed in the fire, begins. You are almost to Pipeline Road, the turnaround point. Retrace your steps for an easy, downhill return to the trailhead.

23 Cañon de Valle

Type of hike: Out-and-back.
Distance: 5.6 miles, round trip.
Elevation change: 1,200 feet.
Maps: Frijoles (USGS), Bland (USGS), Hiking Trails and Jeep Roads of Los Alamos County, Bandelier National Monument and Vicinity (Otowi Station Science Museum Shop and Book Store, Los Alamos), Santa Fe National Forest (USFS).

Finding the trailhead: From Santa Fe take U.S. Highways 285/84 north to Pojoaque. At Pojoaque take Highway 502 west, following signs to Los Alamos, approximately 12 miles to the junction with Highway 4. Follow Highway 4 for approximately 31 miles (passing the entrance to Bandelier National Monument) to the intersection of Highway 501. Turn right (north) and drive 1.3 miles, then turn left (west) onto dirt road 2996 and into a small parking area. The trailhead for Cañon de Valle, Trail 289, lies to the southwest past a metal gate and fence.

The Hike

Although there is a substantial elevation gain on this hike, it is for the most part a pleasant, gentle trail along the canyon bottom, adjacent to a small stream. The trail could be problematic after a heavy rain, however, as there are numerous stream crossings, and the trail is likely to wash out in spots. We met a friendly hiking group from Los Alamos and two mountain bikers, but the appearance of the trail indicated little use.

The first portion of this hike is along a wide, rocky, seldom-used road lined with ponderosa pine, Gambel oak, and mixed conifers. After about 0.7 mile continue straight

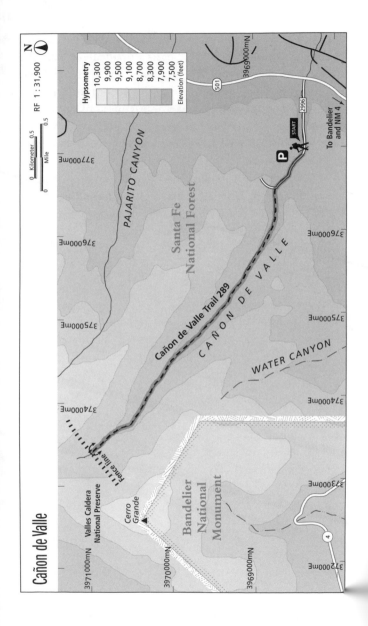

Cañon de Valle

N

| 0 Kilometer | 0.5 | RF 1 : 31,900 |
| 0 | Mile | 0.5 |

Hypsometry
10,300
9,900
9,500
9,100
8,700
8,300
7,900
7,500
Elevation (feet)

3969000mN

501

2996

PAJARITO CANYON

START

P

To Bandelier
and NM 4

3770000mE

Santa Fe
National Forest

CAÑON DE VALLE

3760000mE

Cañon de Valle Trail 289

3755000mE

WATER CANYON

3750000mE

Fence line

3740000mE

Valles Caldera
National Preserve

Cerro
Grande

3971000mN

Bandelier
National
Monument

3970000mN

3969900mN

3730000mE

4

3720000mE

ahead (northwest) on a narrow trail while the road ascends to the right (north). You will begin a gradual ascent as the trail widens then narrows. Several easy creek crossings and the lush riparian vegetation make this section of the hike, along the bottom of the canyon, pleasant, cool, and interesting. After about 2 miles a steeper ascent begins on the northeast side of the canyon, and you lose the stream with the higher ground.

The trail's end is marked by three metal poles immediately followed by a fence, indicating the boundary of the Valles Caldera National Preserve, one of the largest volcanic calderas in the world. There is no trespassing beyond this point. Your return to the trailhead is an easy downhill trek.

Valles Caldera National Preserve

The Valles Caldera was formed over six million years ago by a series of volcanic eruptions that ejected a volume of materials five hundred times greater than the May 1980 eruption of Mount Saint Helens. The volcanic ash covered more than 100 square miles and created the canyons and mesa landscape surrounding Bandelier and Los Alamos.

The caldera created by this activity is more than 16 miles in diameter and is now contained within the 89,000 acres of the Valles Caldera National Preserve. The preserve is a unique venture of the federal government, which purchased the historic Baca Land Grant in 2000 and converted it to public use.

Hiking in the Valles Caldera National Preserve is in its beginning stages of development. The goal of the preserve is to maintain pristine scenery, solitude, and wildlife viewing for each hiker. Therefore, the policy of the preserve includes limiting the number of hikers, creating trails that vary in length, location, and ability, while minimizing the environmental impact on wildlife and cultural resources. To facilitate these goals there are restrictions, which include the use of advance reservations for most hikes, fees, and a shuttle service for visitors wishing to hike.

We have included the two hikes that do not fall into this restricted category. Neither require advance registration, fees, or a shuttle. Please note that the trails are open seven days a week, sunrise to sunset, and pets are not allowed. If you have any inquiries regarding trails or wish to make reservations, you may contact Valles Calderas National Preserve at (505) 661–3333, (866) 382–5537, or www.valles caldera.gov.

24 Valle Grande Trail

Type of hike: Out-and-back.
Distance: 2 miles, round trip.
Elevation change: 481 feet.

Maps: Bland (USGS), Valles
Caldera National Preserve No-
Fee Hiking Trail Map.

Finding the trailhead: From Santa Fe drive north on U.S. Highways 84/285. In Pojoaque follow signs for Los Alamos and Highway
502. Drive through Los Alamos, taking Trinity Drive to Diamond Drive.
Turn left on Diamond, cross the bridge, and then turn right on West
Jemez Road. Drive to the intersection with Highway 4 (note the old
security gate on the right, a reminder of the time when Los Alamos
was a closed city). Turn right, following Highway 4 up and into the
Jemez Mountains for 6.8 miles. Shortly after mile marker 43 there is
a parking area on the left side of the road. The trailhead for the Valle
Grande Trail is across the highway. The trail heads west along the
fence line for a short time before you reach the registration book and
the entrance gate.

The Hike

As a no-reservation hike in the Valles Caldera National Preserve, this is short but beautiful, and characteristic of the
Jemez Mountains, with its aspen and mixed conifer forests. It
feels remote, although you may meet other hikers enjoying
the ease of the hike, and the impressive destination, which is
a lovely view of the peaceful grasslands of the Valle Grande.

Proceed through the entrance gate and follow the well-
worn and well-maintained trail as it takes long and gradual
switchbacks, descending to a well-marked destination point
at the edge of the Valles Grande Caldera. Many years ago this
trail was a wagon road, a precursor to Highway 4. Return on
the same trail, gradually ascending to the trailhead.

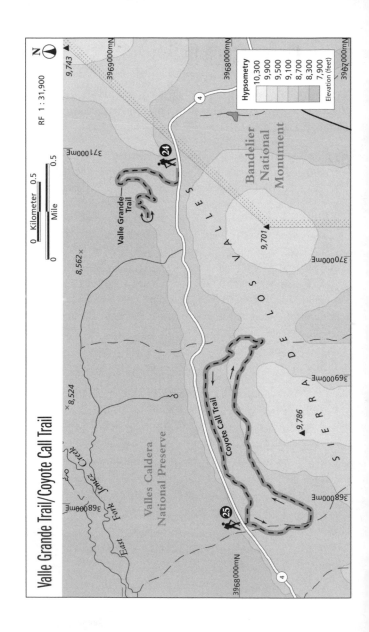

Valle Grande Trail/Coyote Call Trail

RF 1 : 31,900

Hypsometry

	10,300
	9,900
	9,500
	9,100
	8,700
	8,300
	7,900

Elevation (feet)

Bandelier National Monument

▲ 9,701

L O S   V A L L E S

S I E R R A   D E

▲ 9,786

Coyote Call Trail

Valles Caldera National Preserve

East Fork Jemez Creek

× 8,524

× 8,562

Valle Grande Trail

9,743 ▲

0   Kilometer   0.5

0   Mile   0.5

25 Coyote Call Trail

Type of hike: Loop.
Distance: 3 miles.
Elevation change: 250 feet.

Maps: Bland (USGS), Valles Caldera National Preserve No-Fee Hiking Trail Map.

Finding the trailhead: From Santa Fe drive north on U.S. Highways 84/285. In Pojoaque follow signs for Los Alamos and Highway 502. Drive through Los Alamos, taking Trinity Drive to Diamond Drive. Turn left on Diamond, cross the bridge, and turn right on West Jemez Road. Drive to the intersection with Highway 4 (note the abandoned security gate from the old "secret city"). Turn right, following Highway 4 up and into the Jemez Mountains for 8.8 miles. A small parking spot, bordering the Valles Caldera, will be on the right (north side of the highway). Park here and cross the road for the trailhead.

The Hike

This is another no reservation, easy hike, offering beautiful views of the Valles Caldera National Preserve, as you walk on a wide trail in the forests of the Jemez Mountains. Keep an occasional eye on the trail beneath you, as there is an abundance of obsidian rock, reminding you of the origins of this unique region.

Be sure to register your hike before walking through the trailhead gate. Follow the old road to your right (south). The faint trail you see to the left is your return route. Notice the brown plastic posts along the trail as you walk uphill. These markers are indicators of a Valles Caldera hike. You will also see blue metal markers on many trees, as this is a cross-country ski trail in winter months.

As the trail climbs it changes direction several times and meanders in a beautiful aspen and conifer meadow. At the top of the hill it heads east (left). Within a few feet you will see a wooden sign, indicating that Coyote Call (Meadow Walk) Trail continues to the left (northeast) and Rabbit Ridge Trail veers to the right. Follow the wonderfully flat, wide road to the left and enjoy the views of the Valles Caldera through several breaks in the trees. At about 1.4 miles you will reach a turnaround point, and you are directed by the brown posts and an orange NO ACCESS sign to take a left turn (north), downhill.

You now have a gentle downhill, zig-zag route, often paralleling the highway below. If it is late spring, you'll be lucky to walk through and past Rocky Mountain flag (wild iris) back to the trailhead.

About the Authors

Katie, Linda, and Jim Regnier live in Montana. Linda was raised in northern New Mexico, where she and Jim return each year to hike and backpack. They are all wilderness enthusiasts and share a deep concern for its preservation. All three devote time and energy volunteering on environmental and conservation issues and urge readers of this book to consider action on the behalf of wilderness.